COMPLETE PROCESS
COLOR FINDER

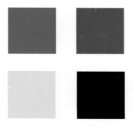

THIS BOOK WAS DESIGNED AND PRODUCED BY:
QUARTO INC.
THE OLD BREWERY
6 BLUNDELL STREET
LONDON N7 9BH

FIRST PUBLISHED IN THE UNITED STATES OF AMERICA BY:
ROCKPORT PUBLISHERS, INC.
146 GRANITE STREET
ROCKPORT, MASSACHUSETTS 01966
TELEPHONE: (508) 546-9590
FAX: (508) 546-7141

DISTRIBUTED TO THE BOOK TRADE AND ART TRADE IN THE U.S. AND CANADA BY:
NORTH LIGHT, AN IMPRINT OF
F & W PUBLICATIONS
1507 DANA AVENUE
CINCINNATI, OHIO 45207
TELEPHONE: (513) 531-2222

OTHER DISTRIBUTION BY:
ROCKPORT PUBLISHERS, INC.
ROCKPORT, MASSACHUSETTS 01966

ISBN 1-56496-134-6

10 9 8 7 6 5 4 3 2 1

COMPLETE PROCESS COLOR FINDER

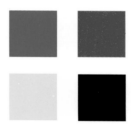

ROCKPORT PUBLISHERS, ROCKPORT, MASSACHUSETTS
DISTRIBUTED BY
NORTHLIGHT BOOKS, CINCINNATI, OHIO

PRINTING SPECIFICATIONS

INK USE : JAPANESE INK QS A-A.

PRINTING SEQUENCE : BLACK CYAN MAGENTA YELLOW

PRINTING MACHINE : KOMORI LITHRONE 40 MADE IN JAPAN

PRINTING SPEED : 11,000 SHEETS PER HOUR

SCREEN TINT USED : 150L/IN

SCREEN ANGLES : BLACK 75°
CYAN 15°
MAGENTA 45°
YELLOW 50°

COLOUR DENSITY: BLACK 1.85
CYAN 1.45
MAGENTA 1.40
YELLOW 1.40

PLATE MATERIAL : POLYCHROME G.P.6 (PS PLATE)

PAPER : PRINTED ON 140GSM JAPANESE TOP KOTE GLOSSY ART PAPER

TOLERANCE LEVEL ON PRINTED PAGES : +3% - -3%

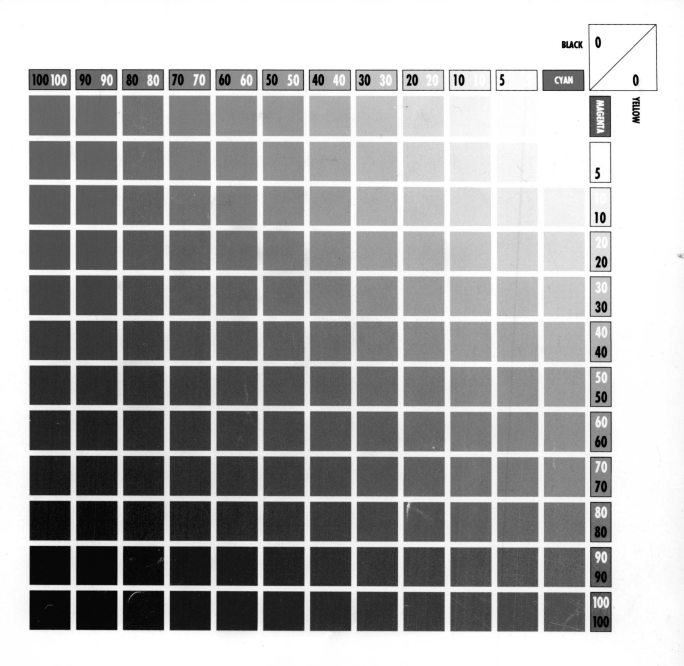

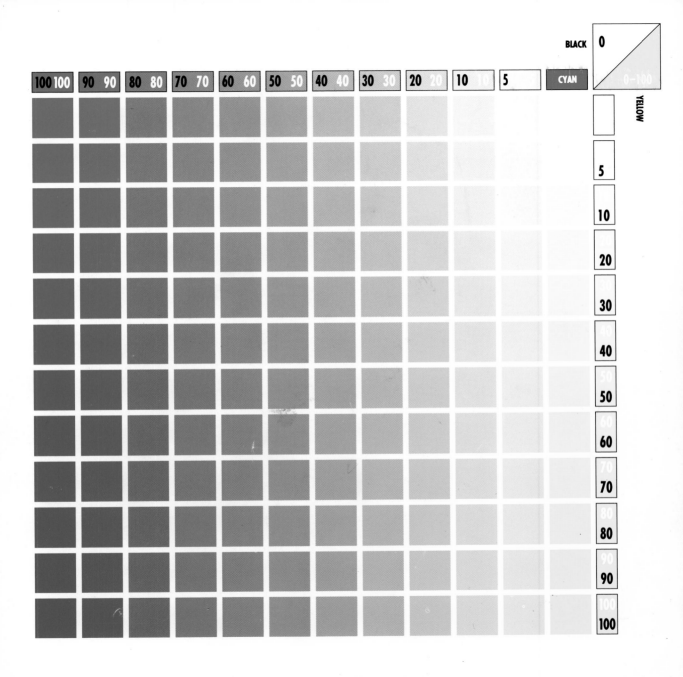

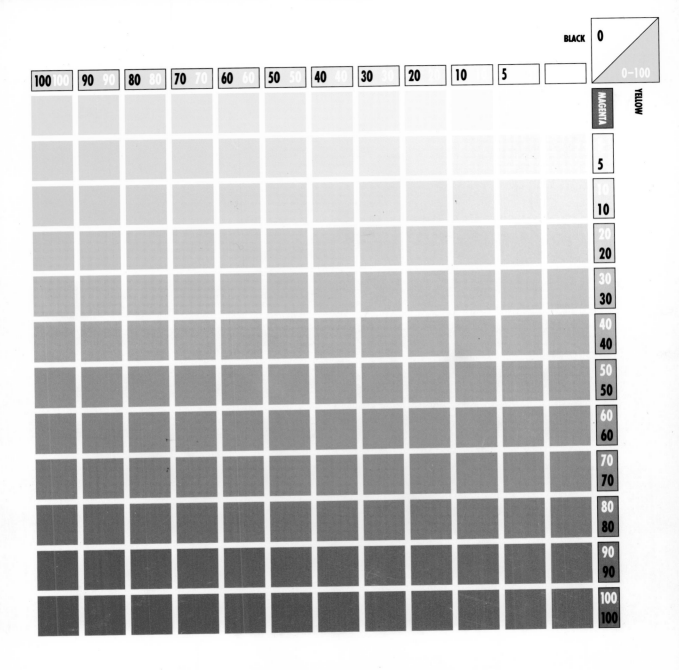

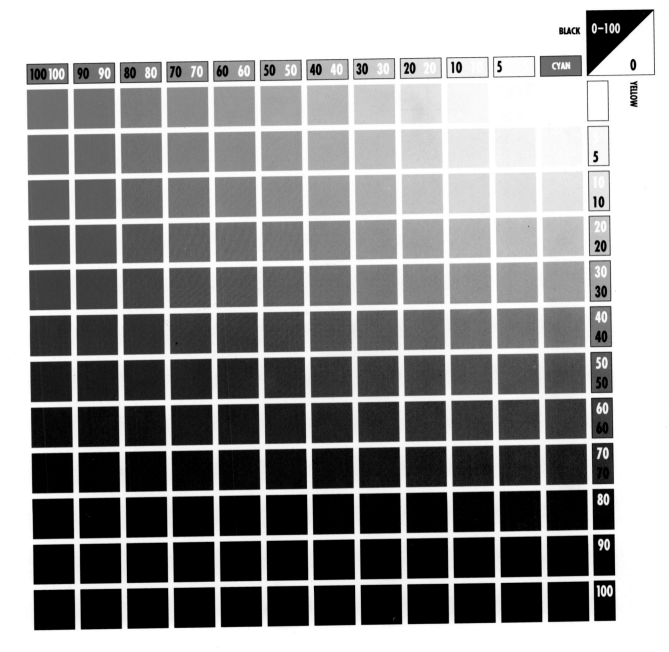

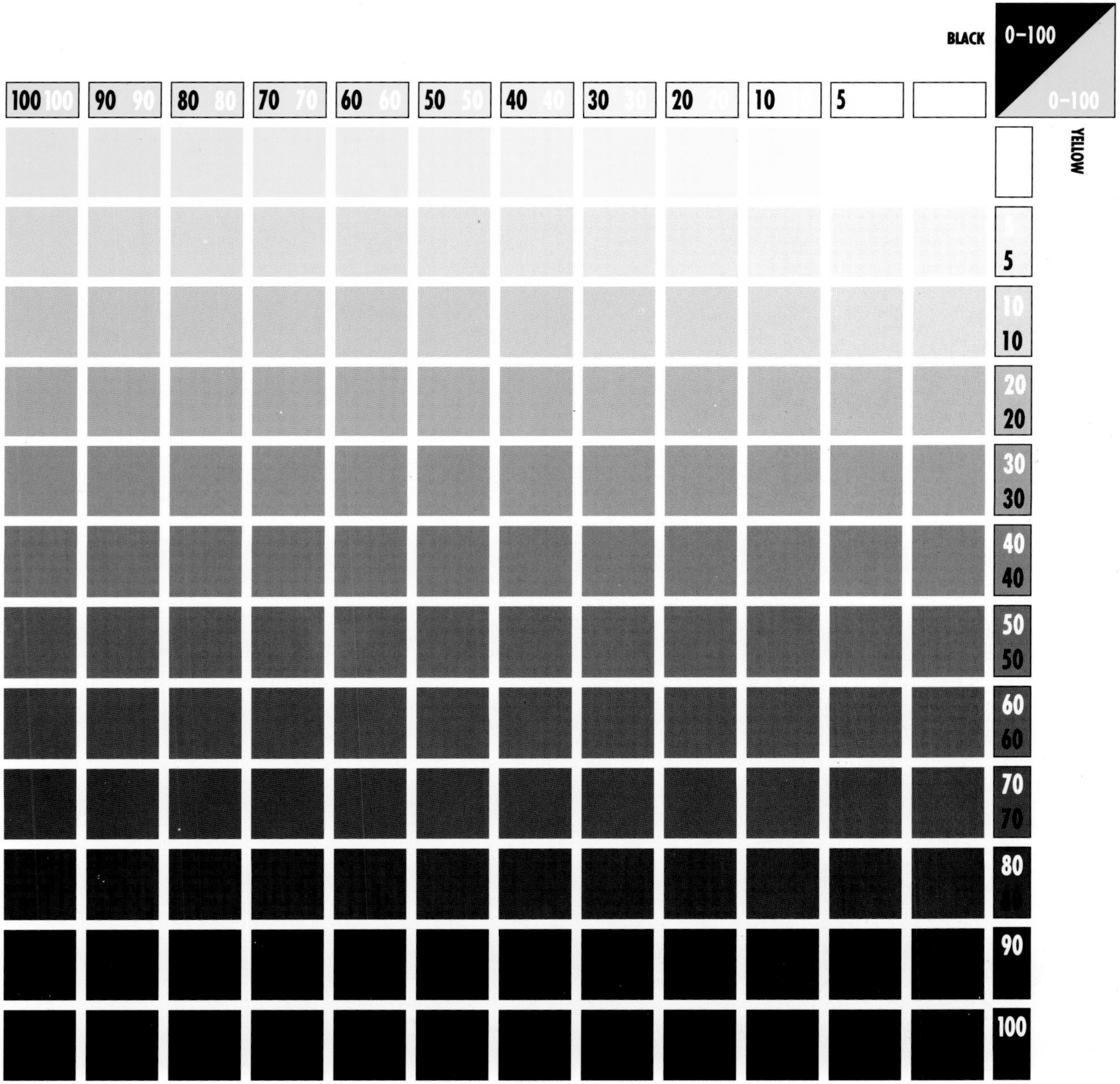
BLACK
0–100
0–100
YELLOW
100
90
80
70
60
50
40
30
20
10
5
5
10
20
30
40
50
60
70
80
90
100

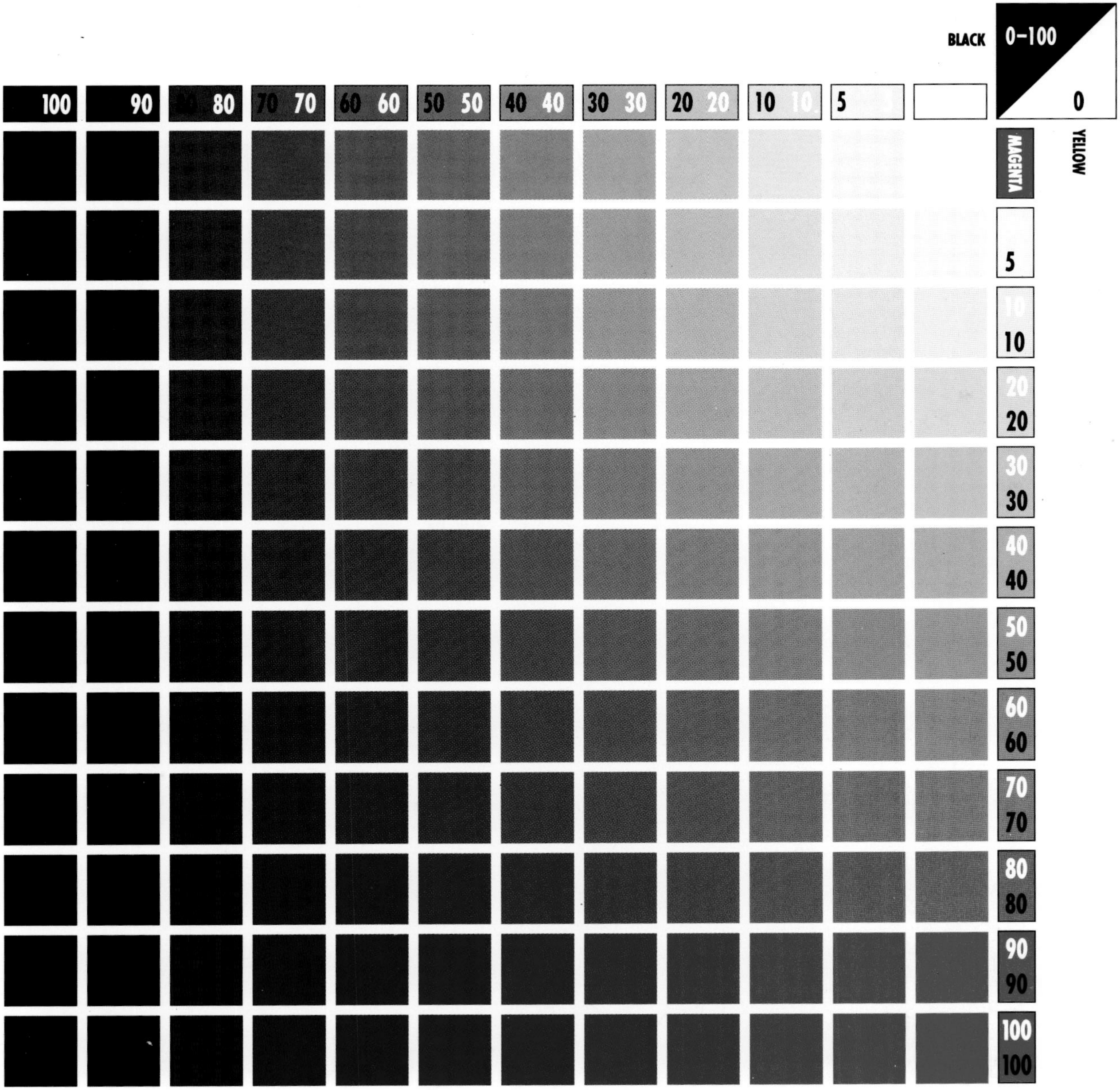
BLACK
0–100
0
MAGENTA
YELLOW
100
90
80
70 70
60 60
50 50
40 40
30 30
20 20
10 10
5
5
10
20
30
40
50
60
70
80
90
100

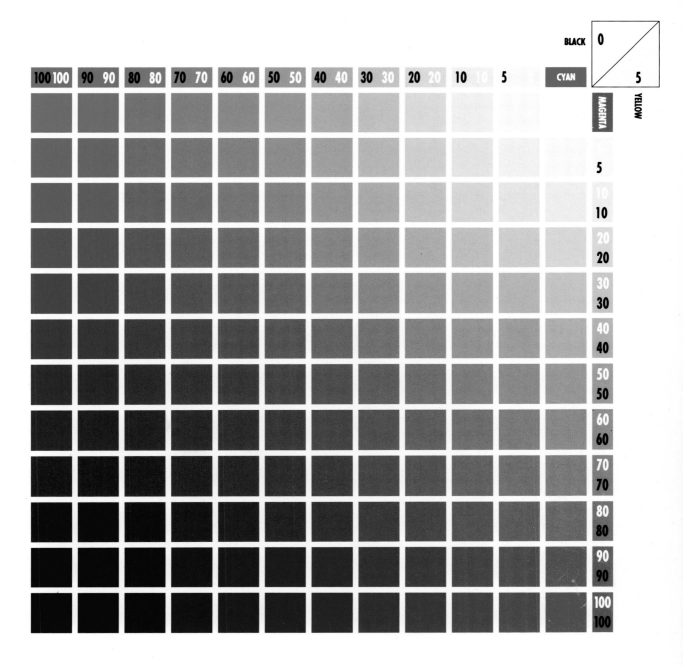

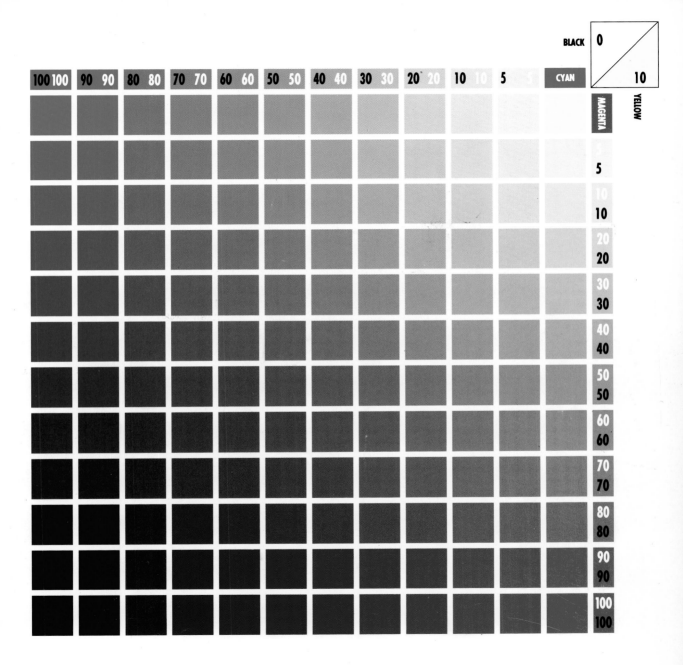

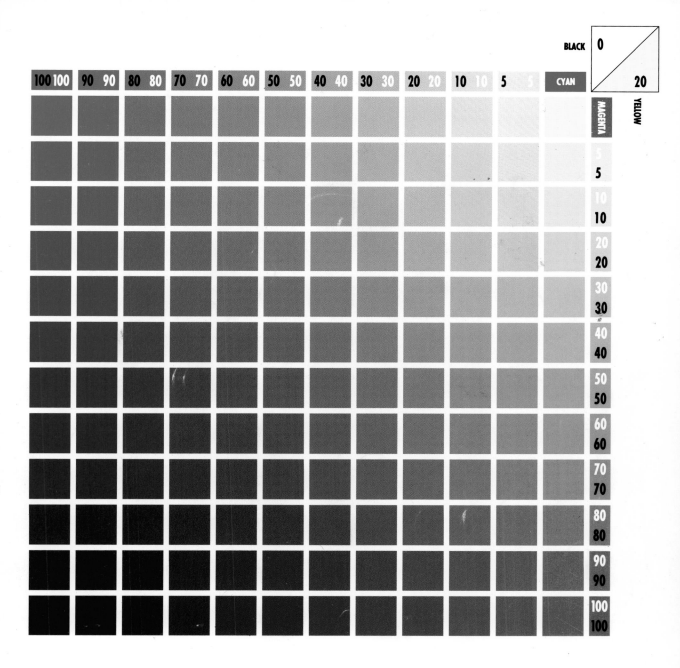

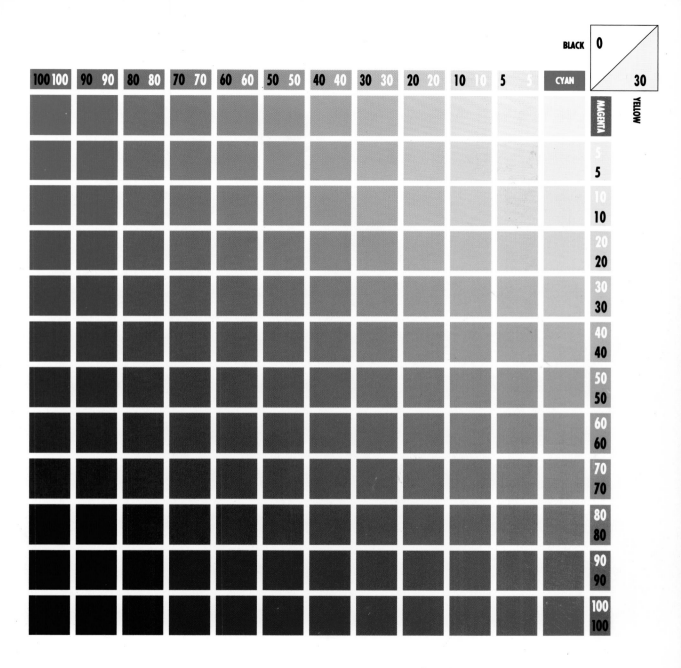

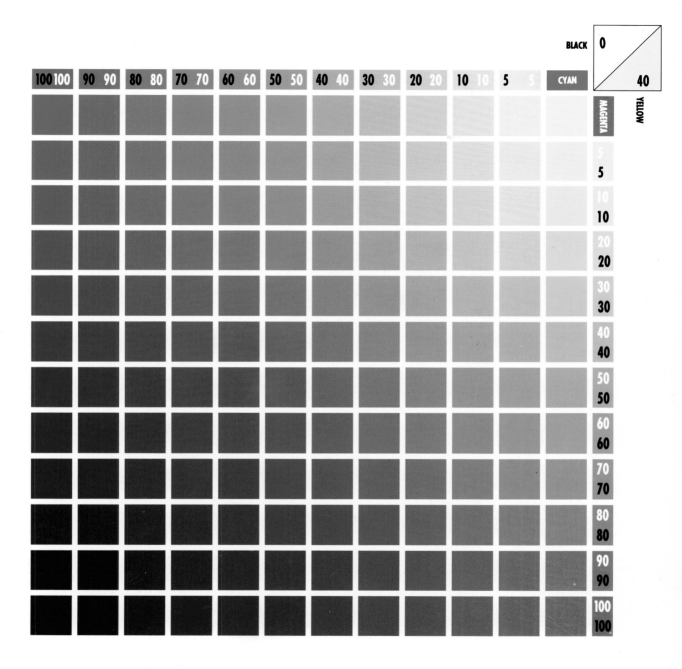

BLACK 0

YELLOW 40

| 100 100 | 90 90 | 80 80 | 70 70 | 60 60 | 50 50 | 40 40 | 30 30 | 20 20 | 10 10 | 5 5 | CYAN | MAGENTA |

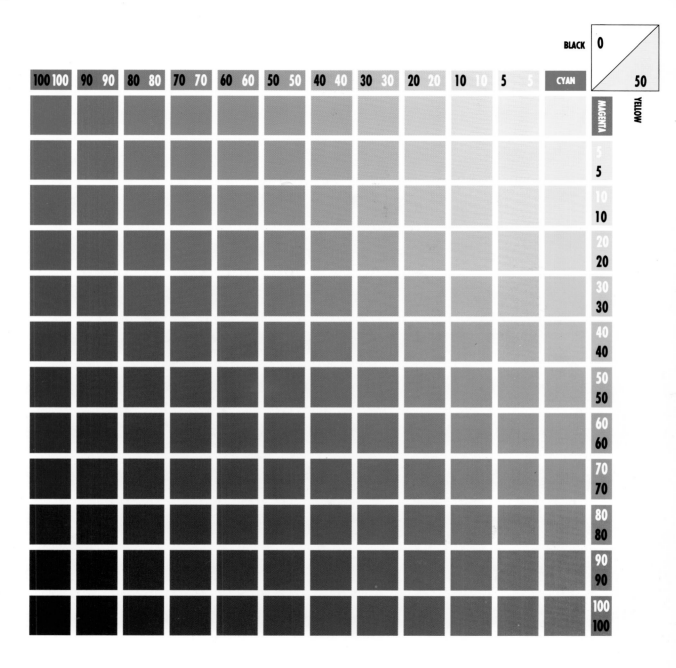

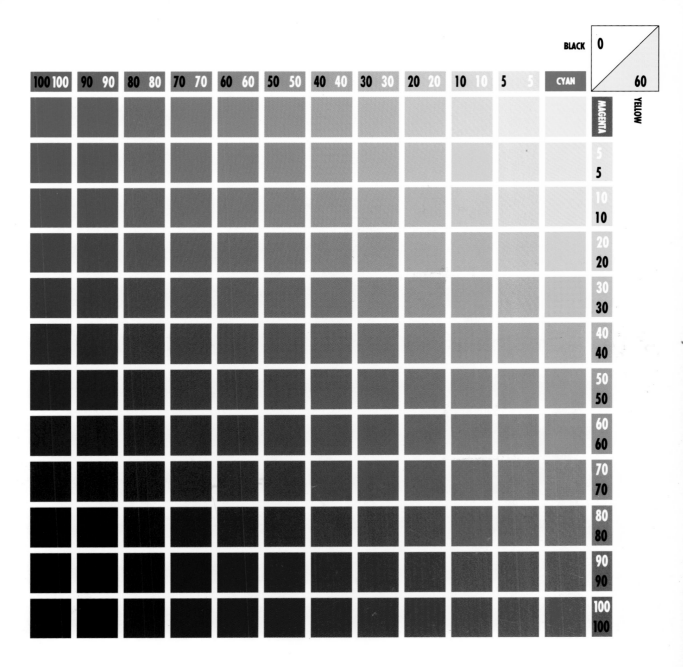

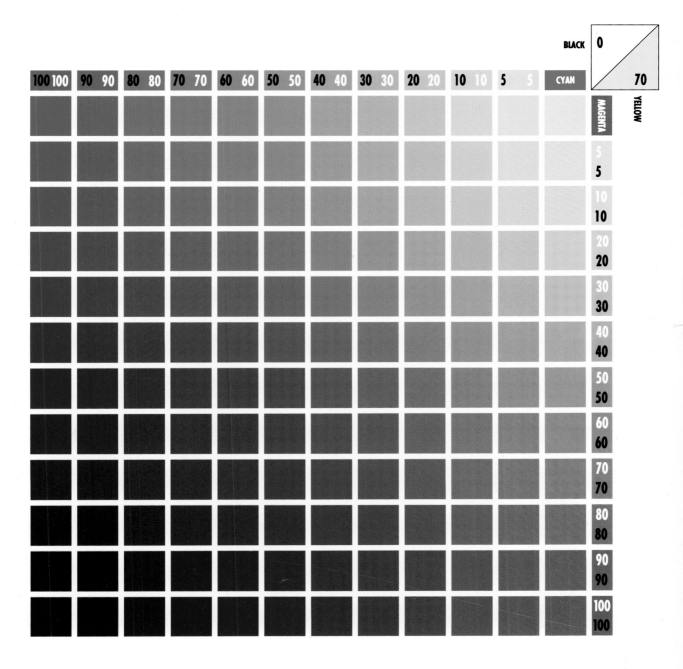

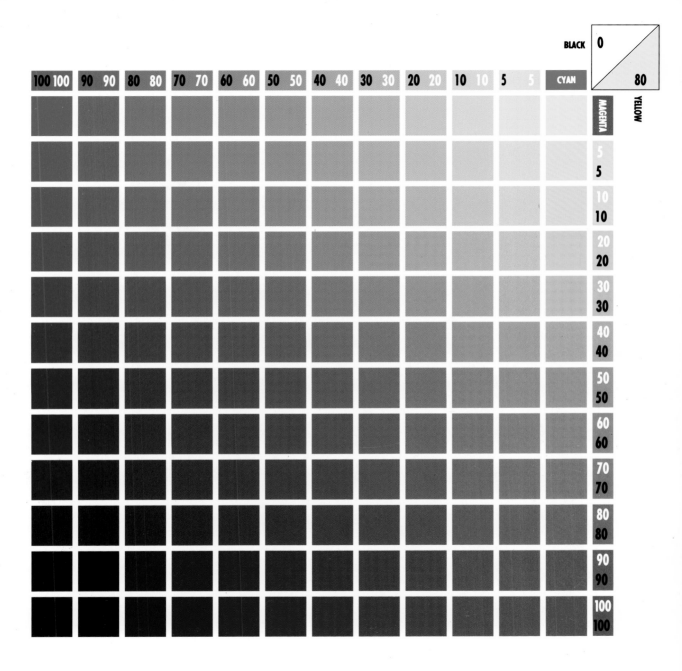

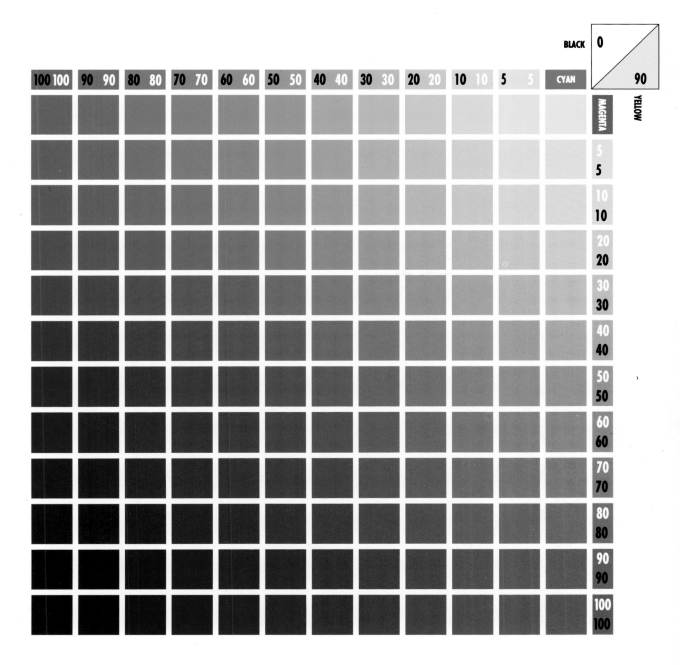

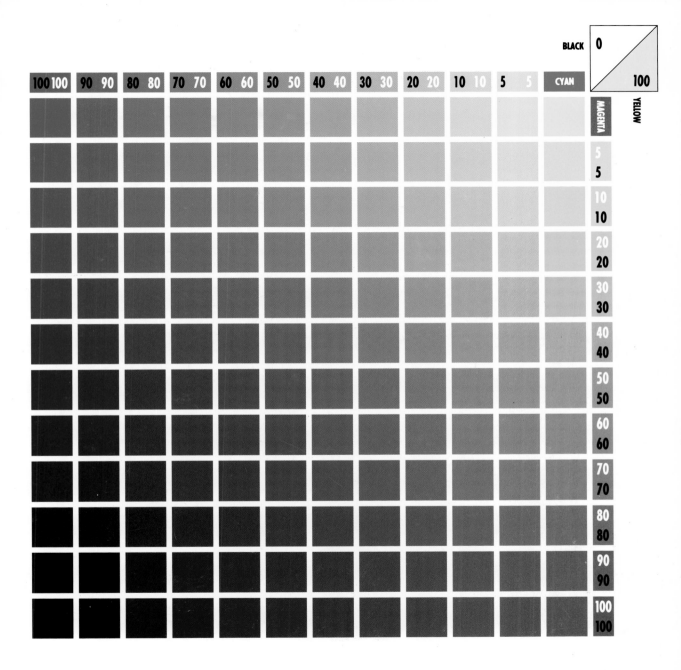

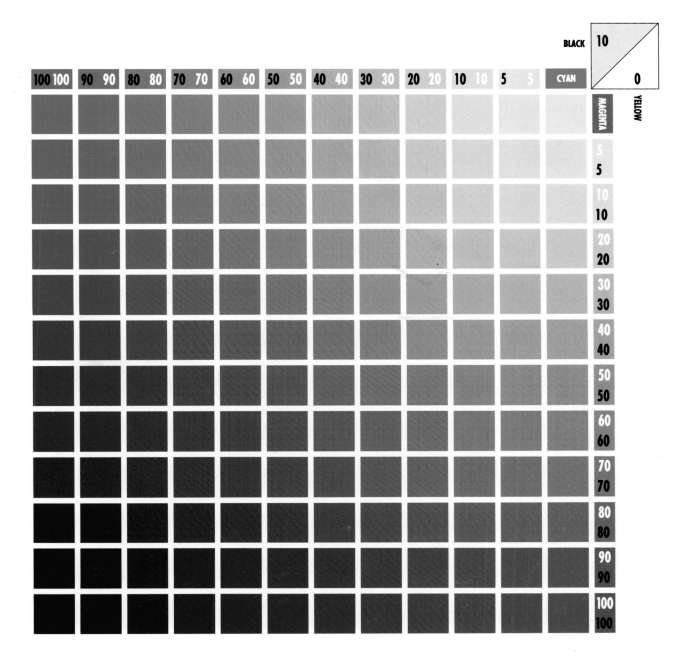

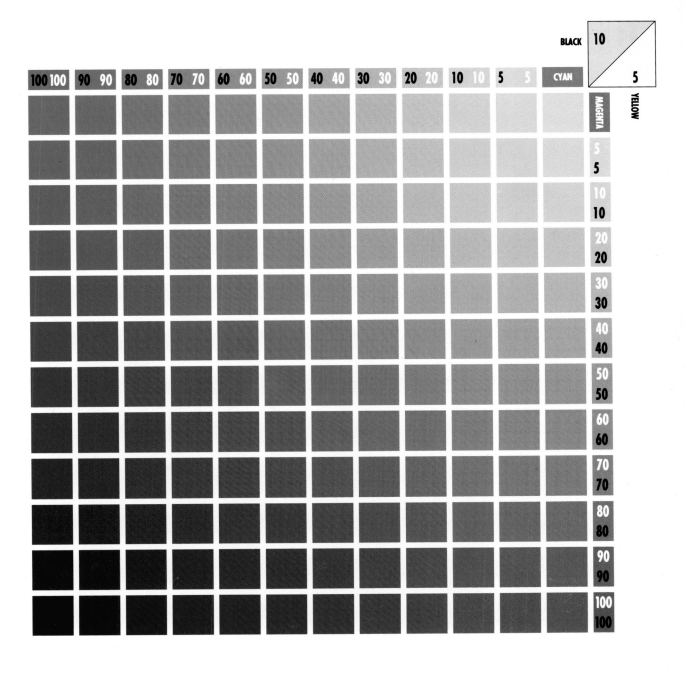

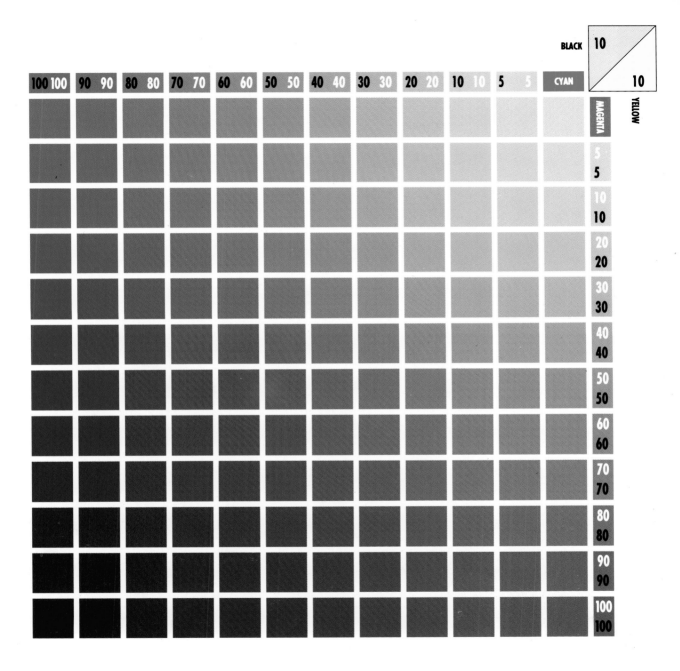

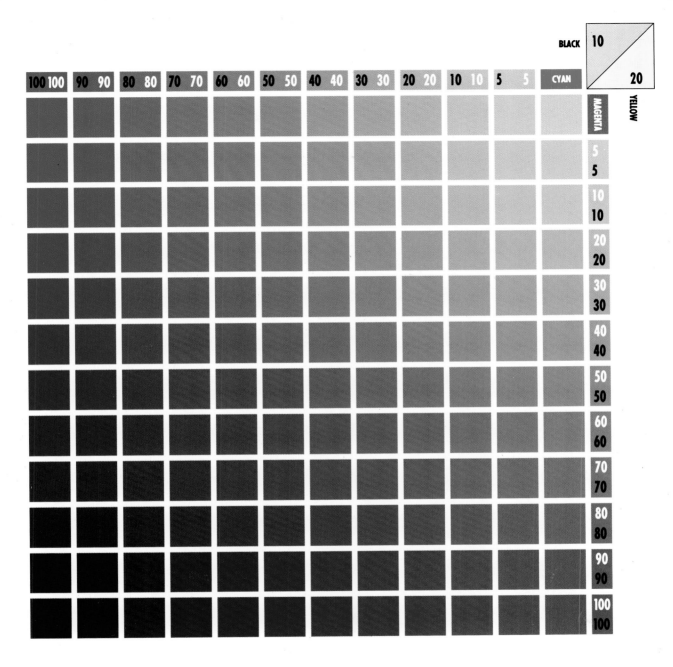

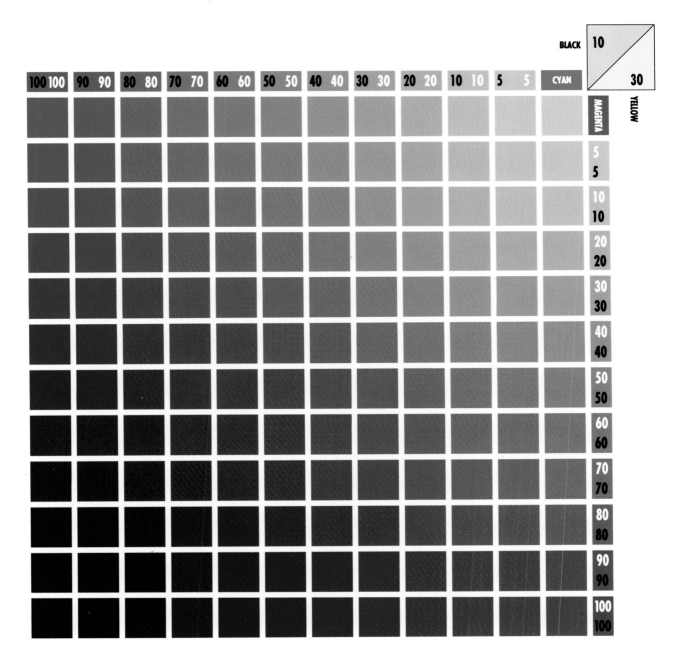

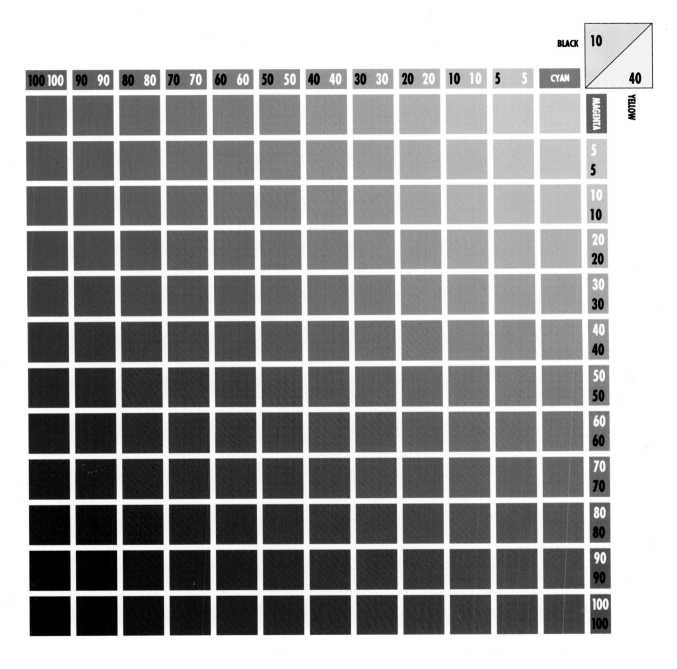

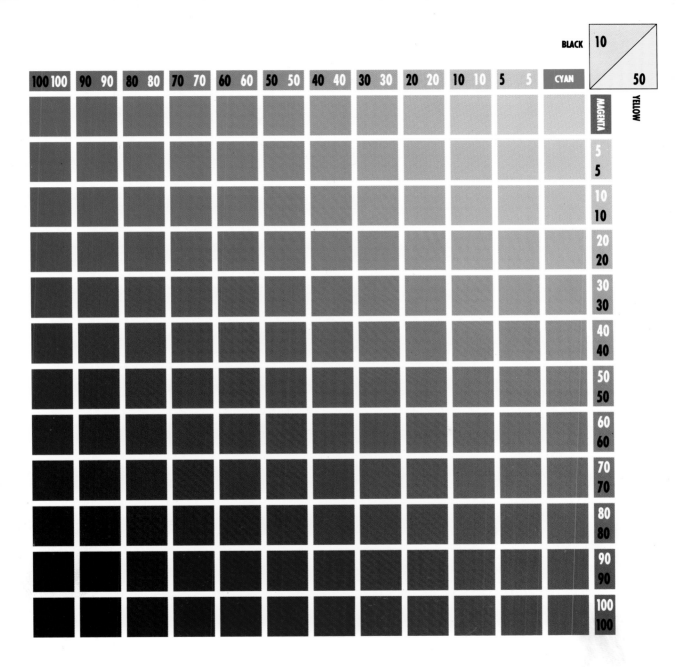

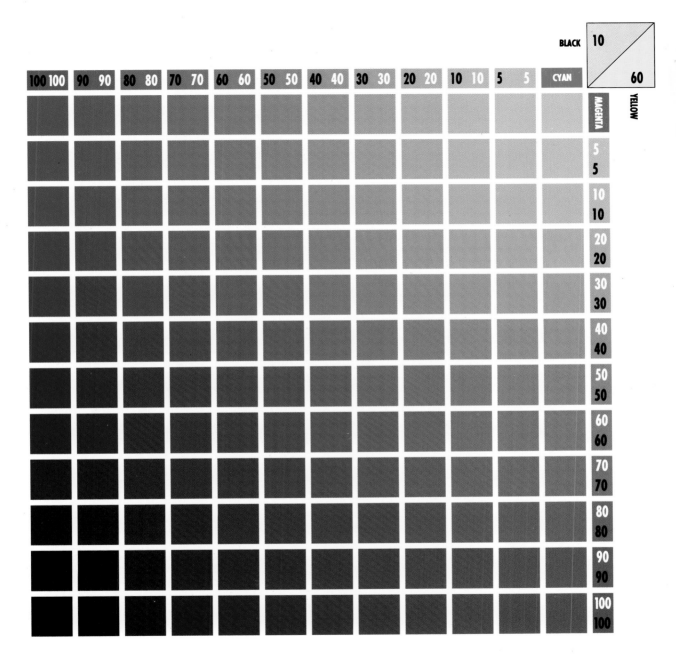

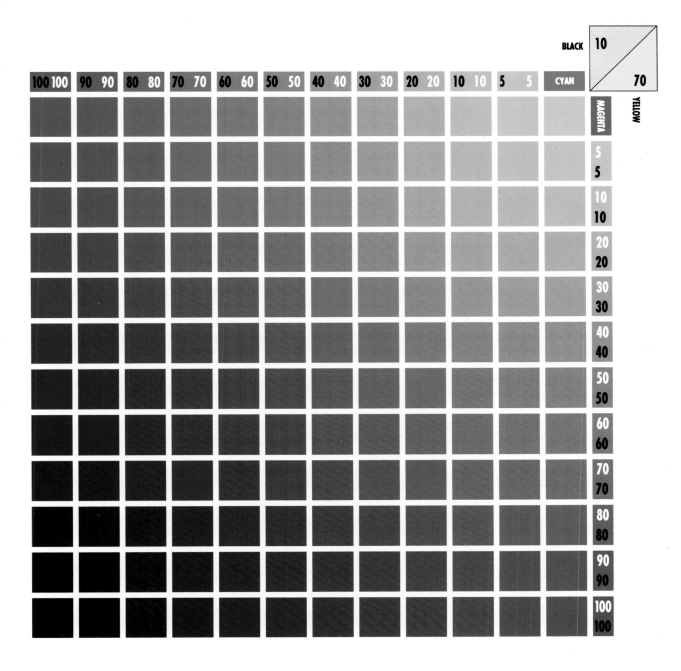

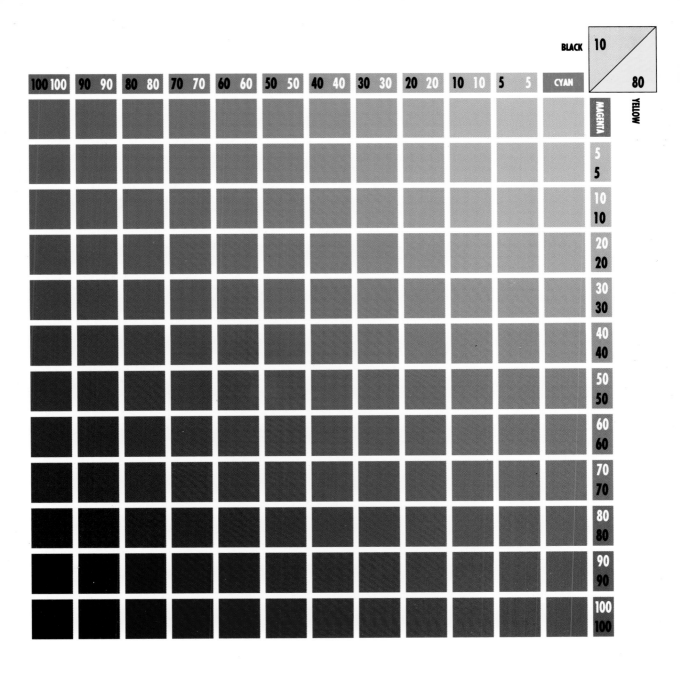

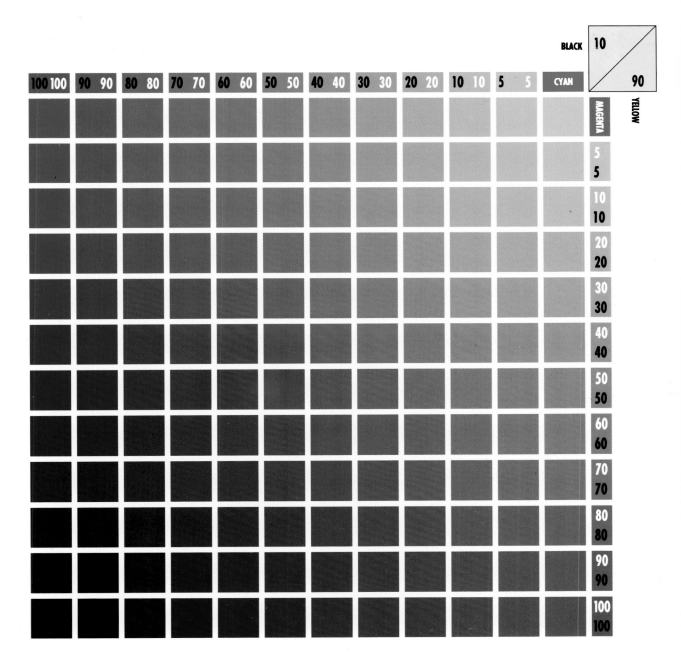

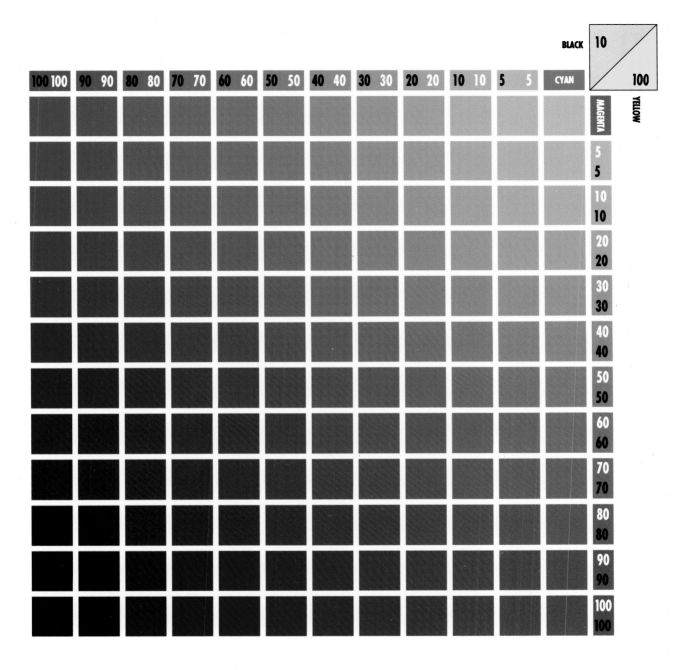

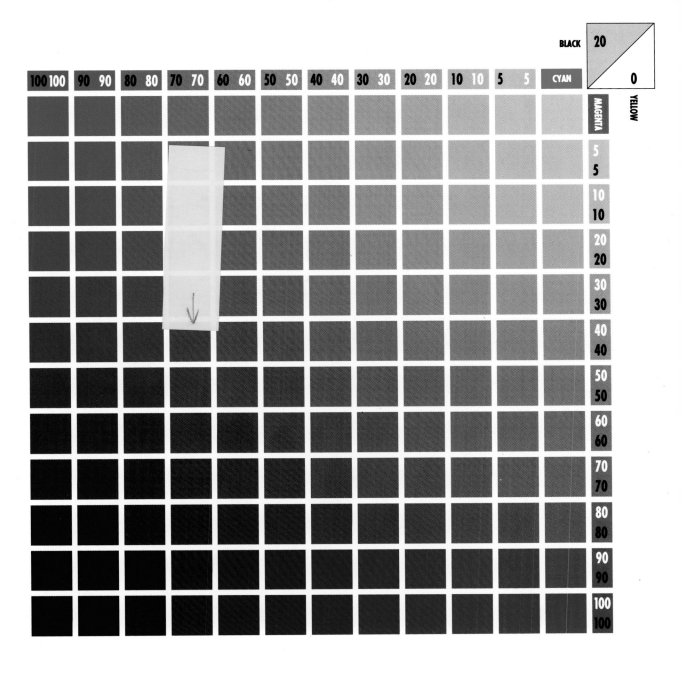

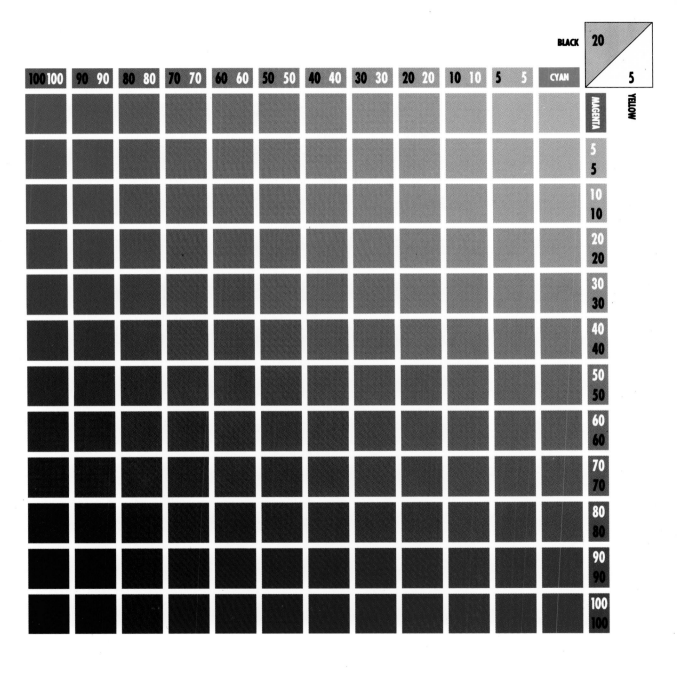

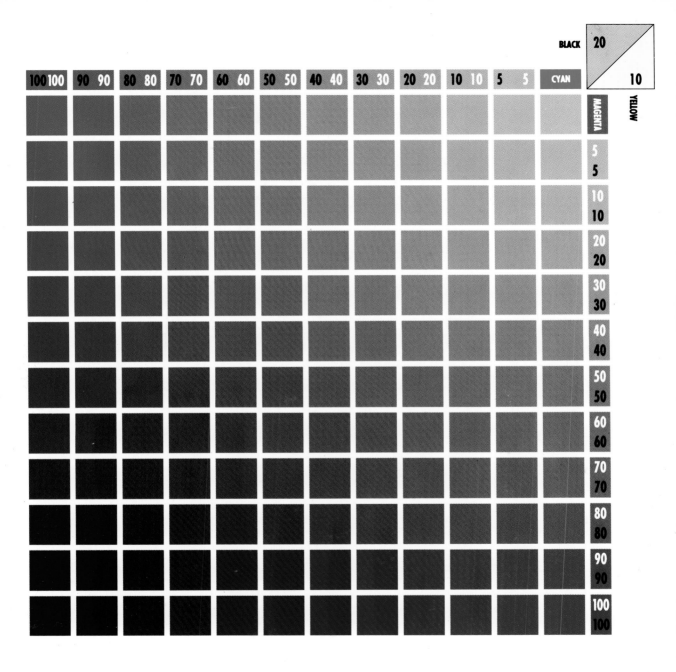

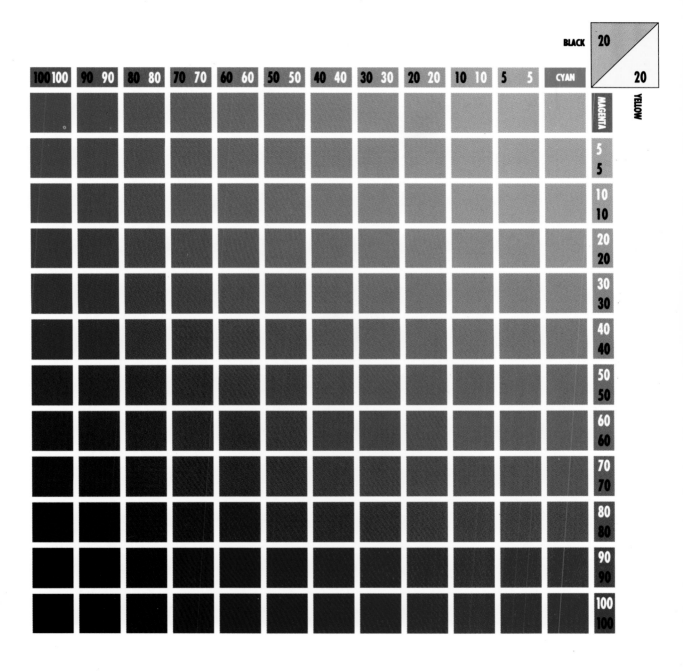

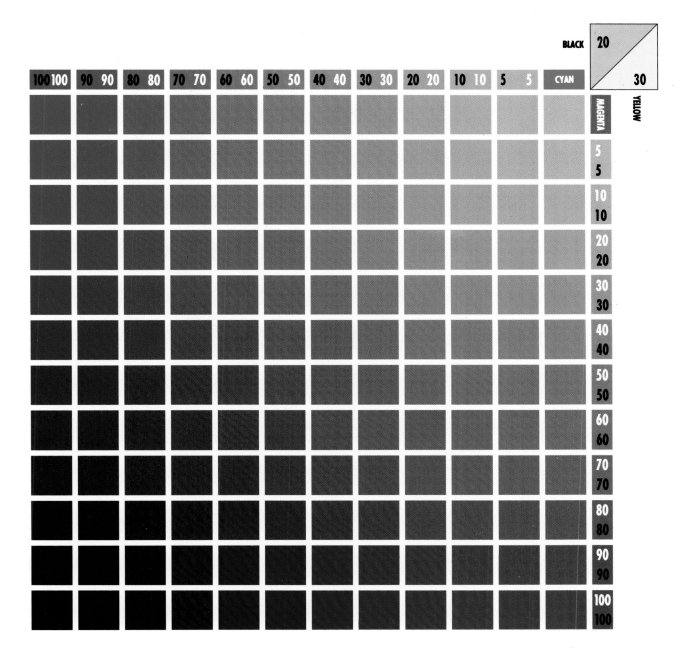

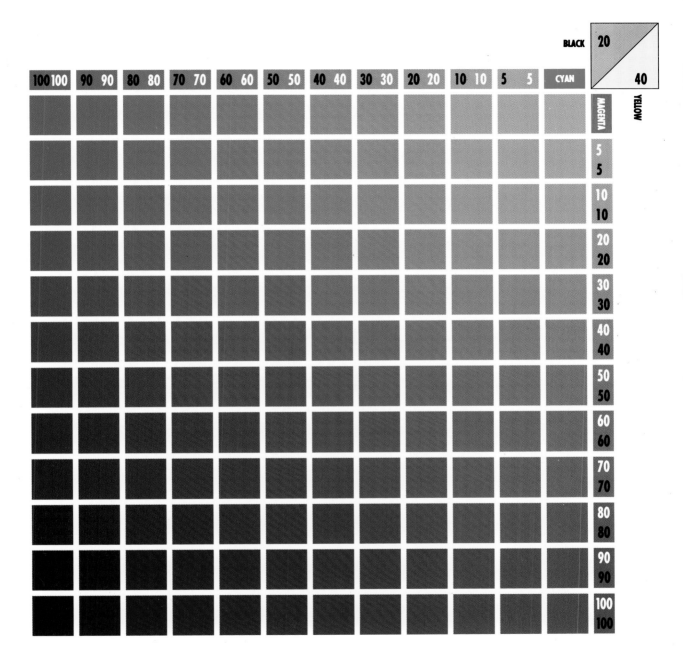

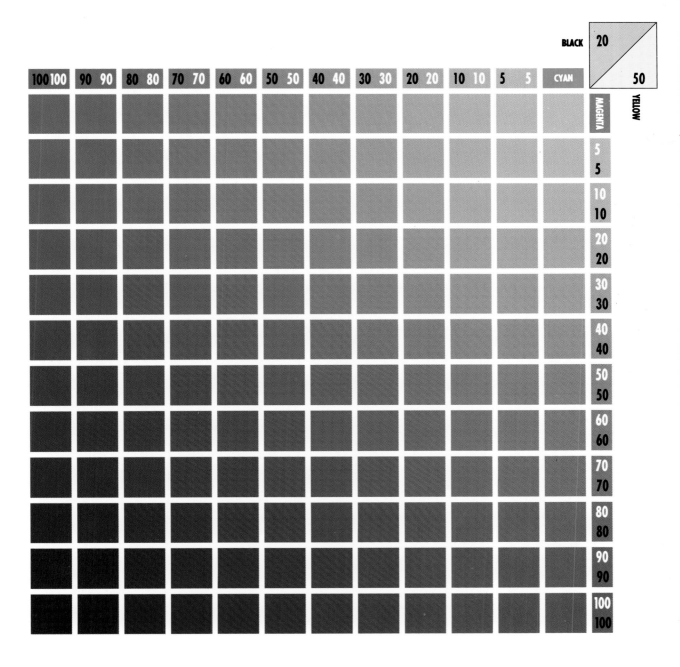

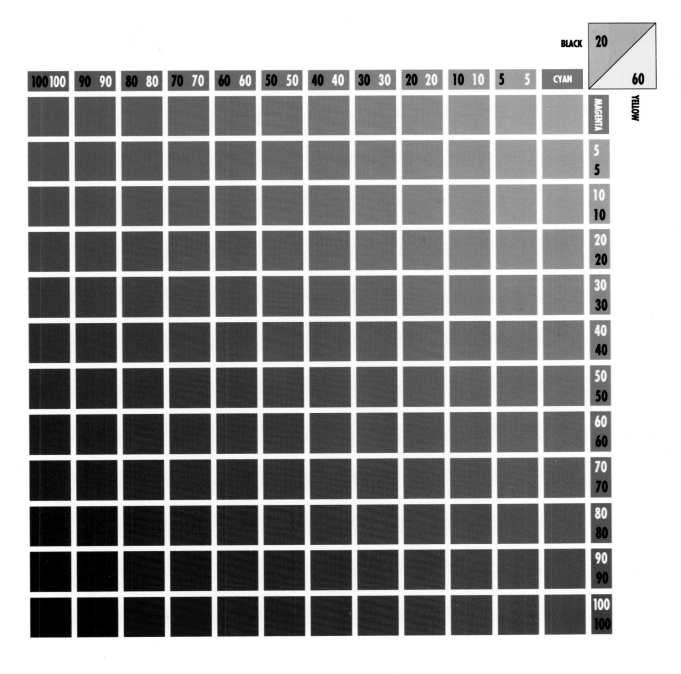

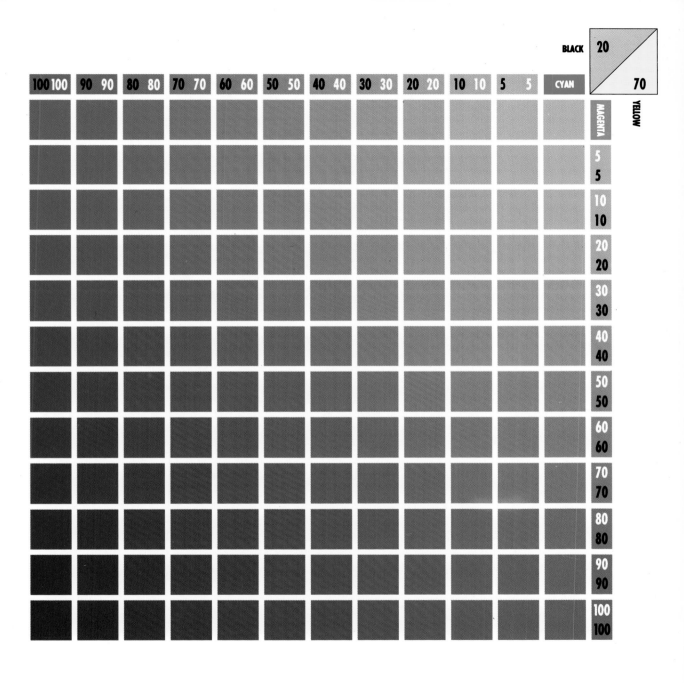

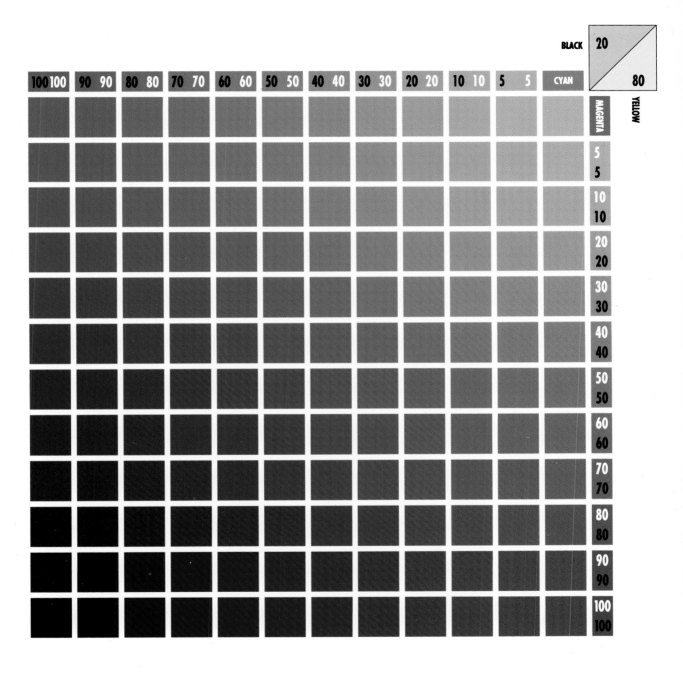

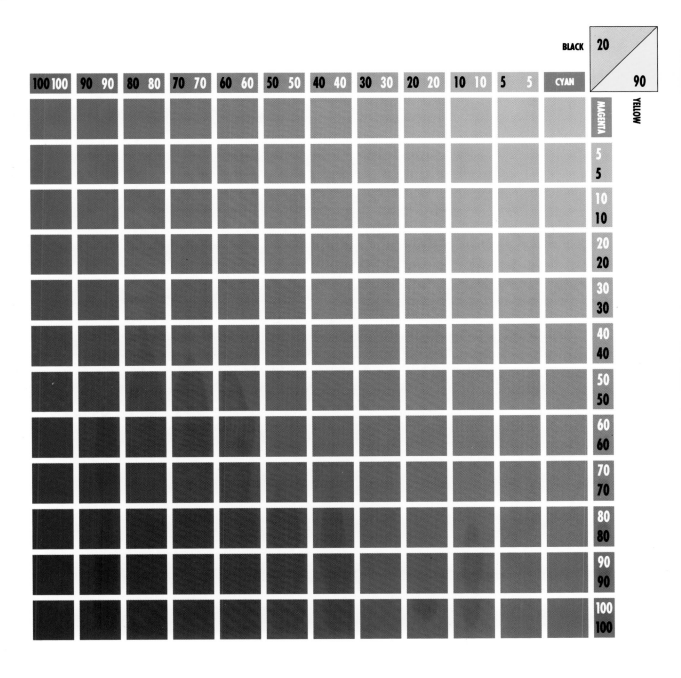

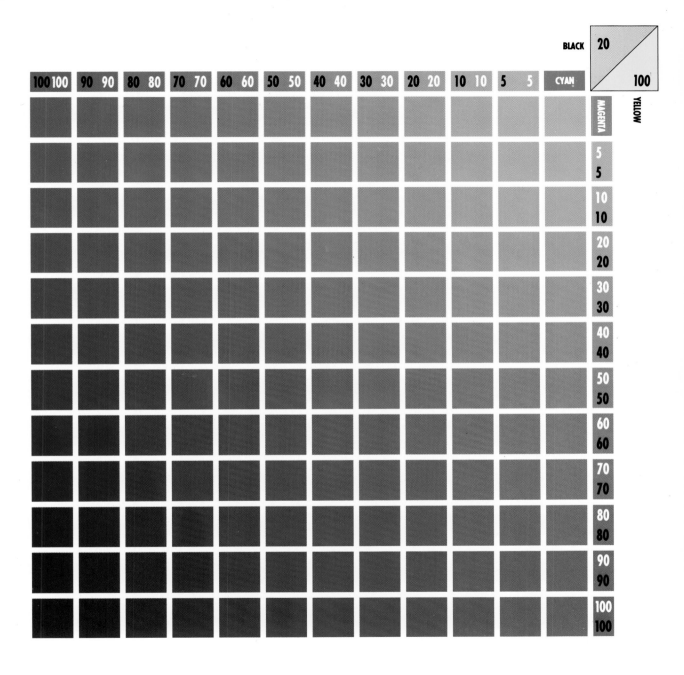

BLACK 30 / 0 YELLOW

| 100 100 | 90 90 | 80 80 | 70 70 | 60 60 | 50 50 | 40 40 | 30 30 | 20 20 | 10 10 | 5 5 | CYAN |

MAGENTA

5 5
10 10
20 20
30 30
40 40
50 50
60 60
70 70
80 80
90 90
100 100

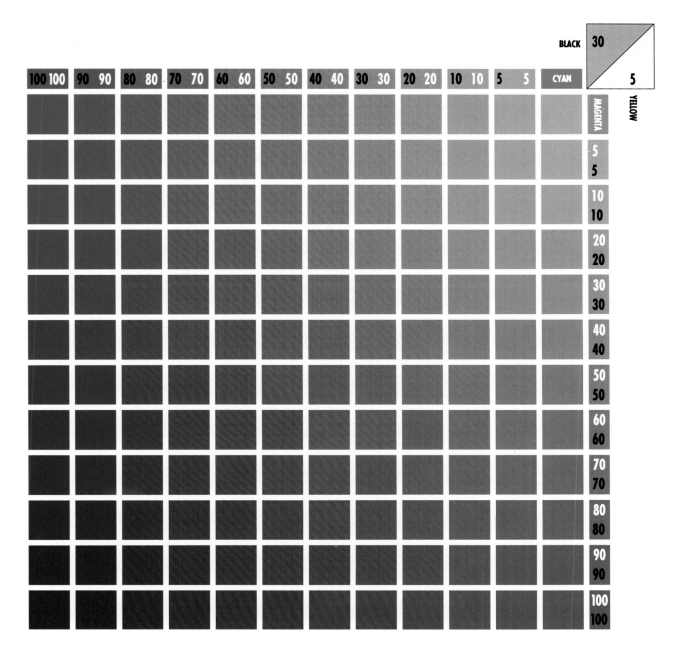

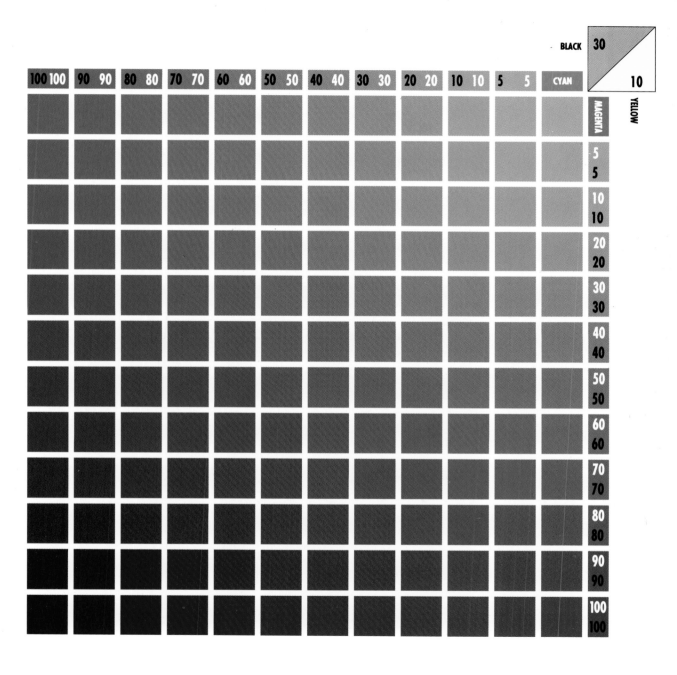

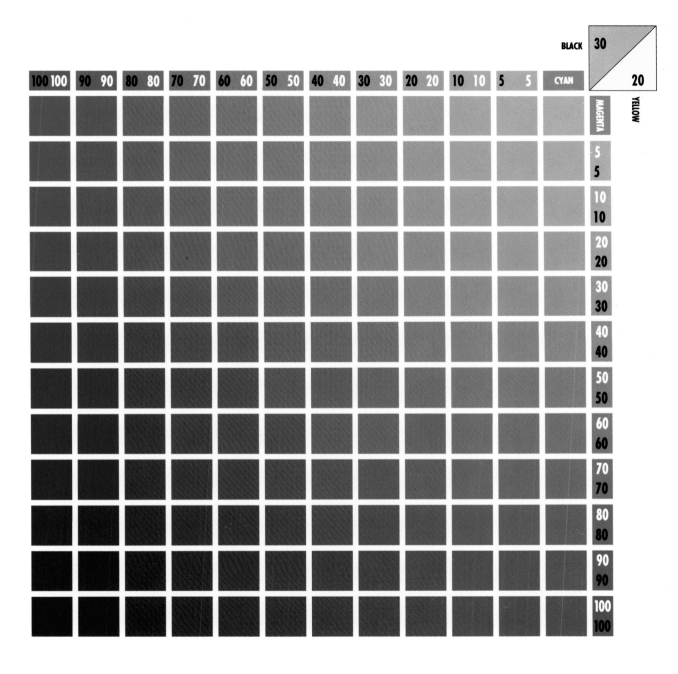

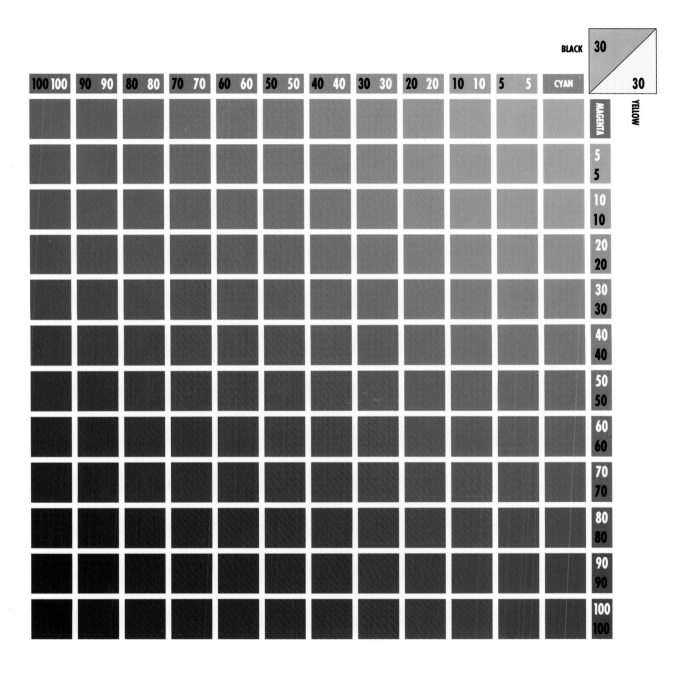

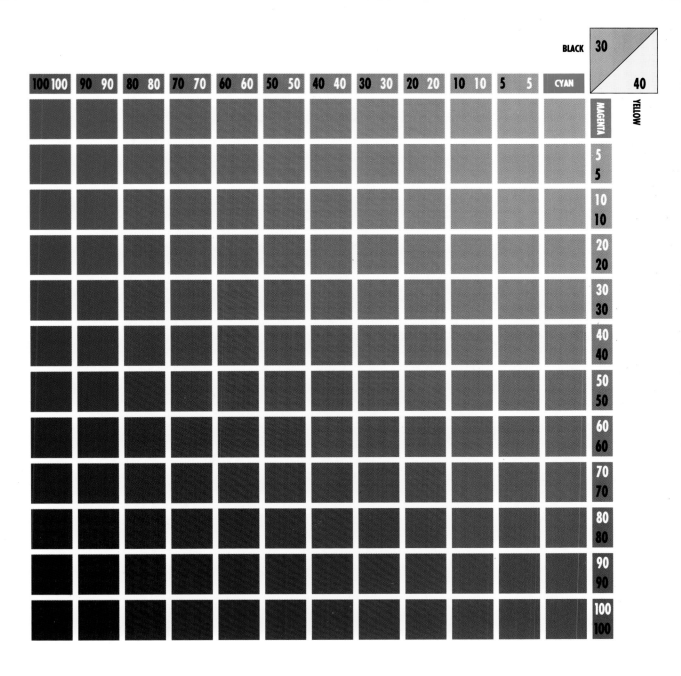

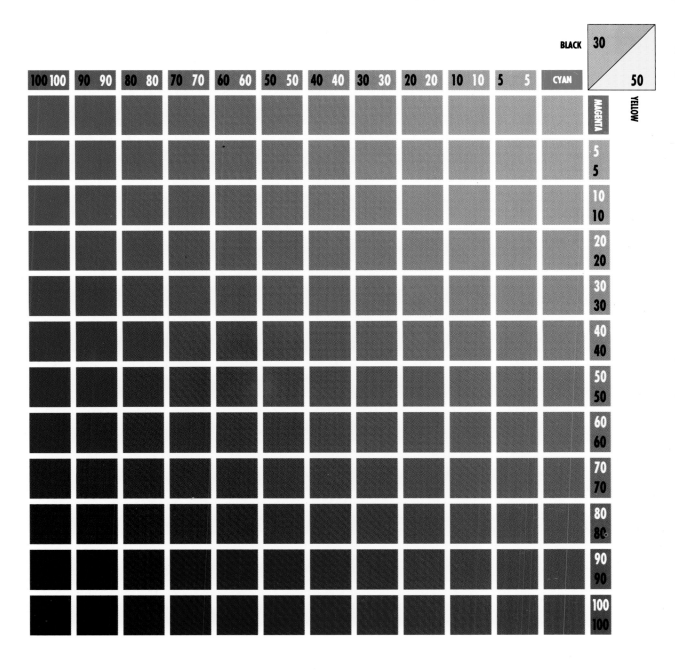

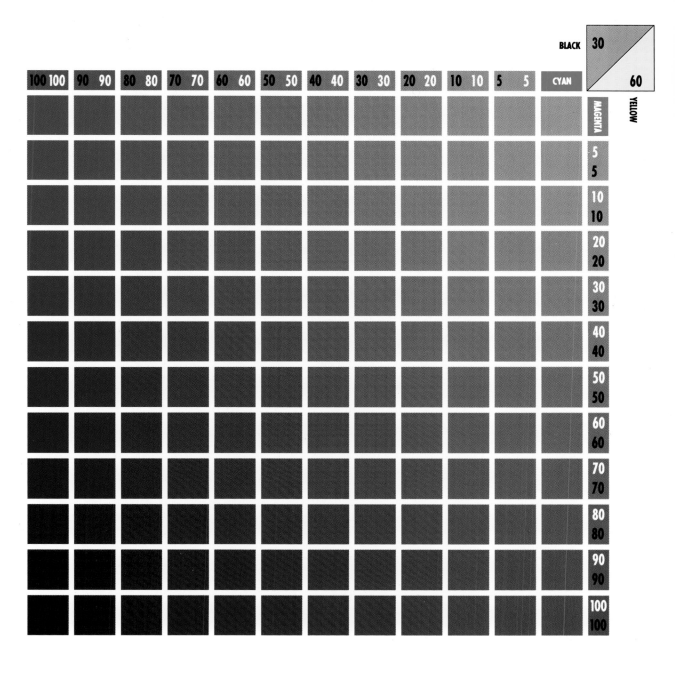

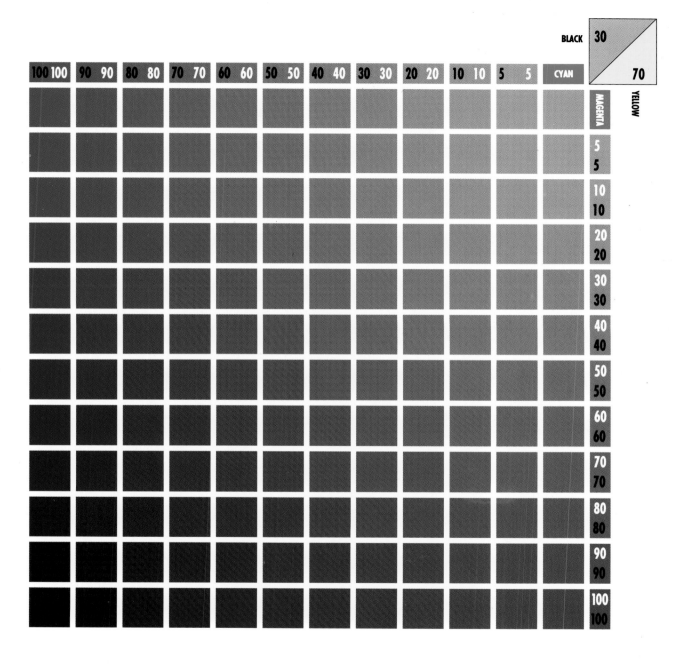

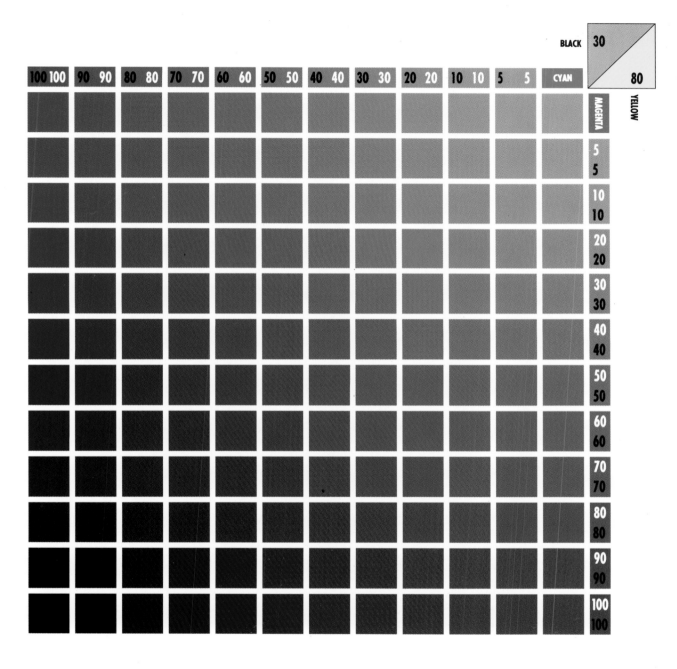

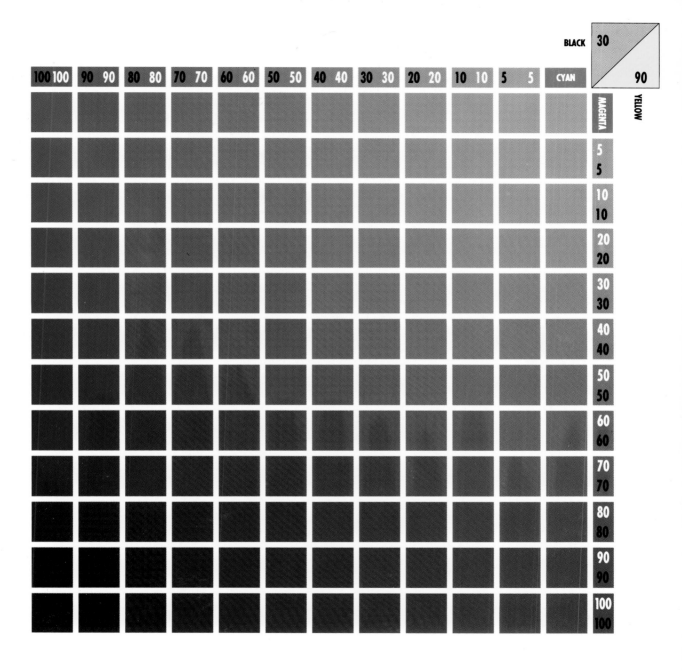

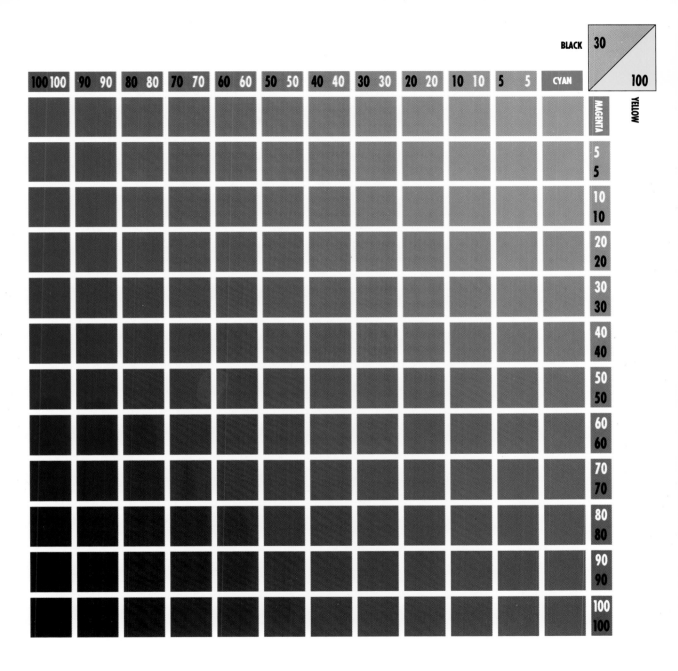

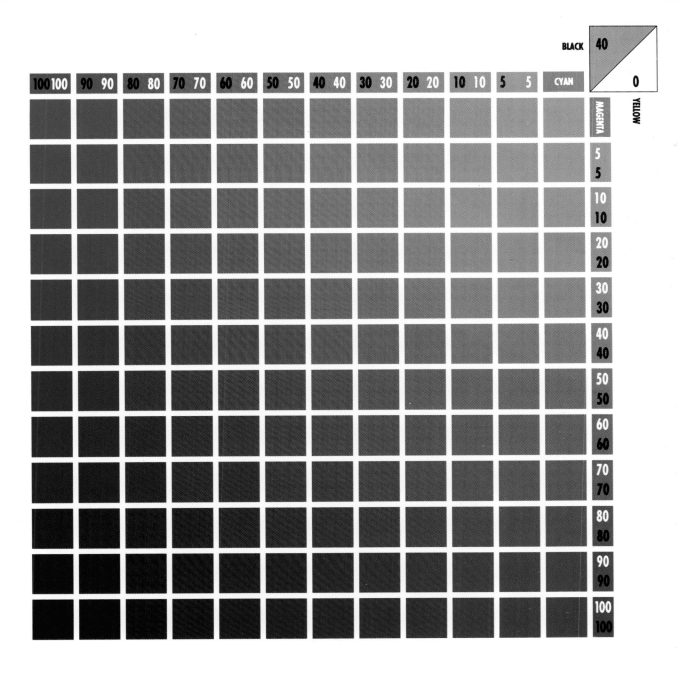

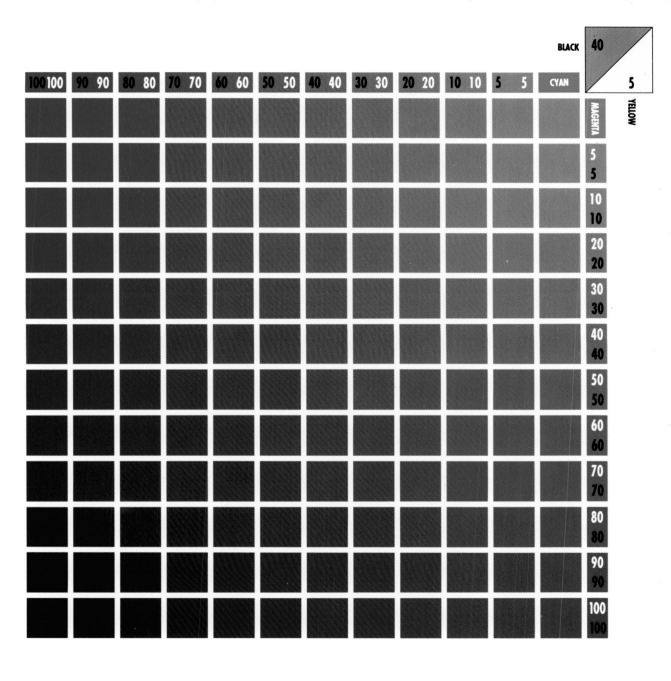

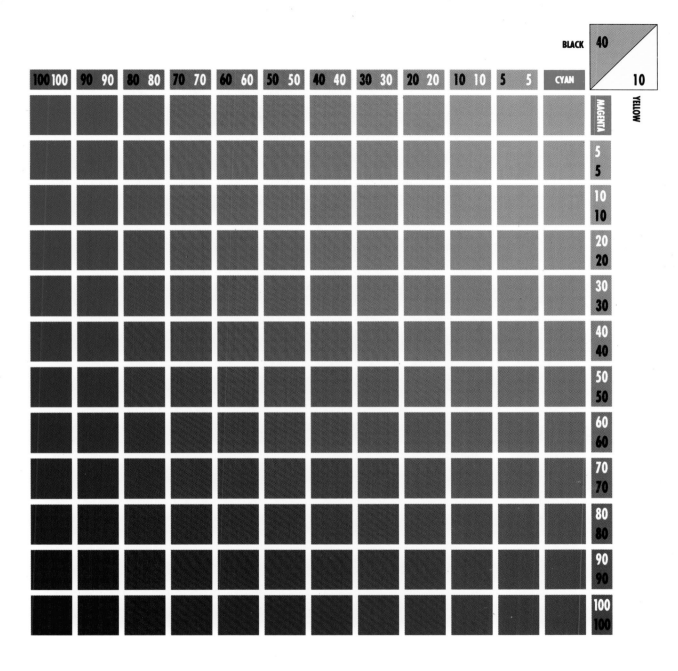

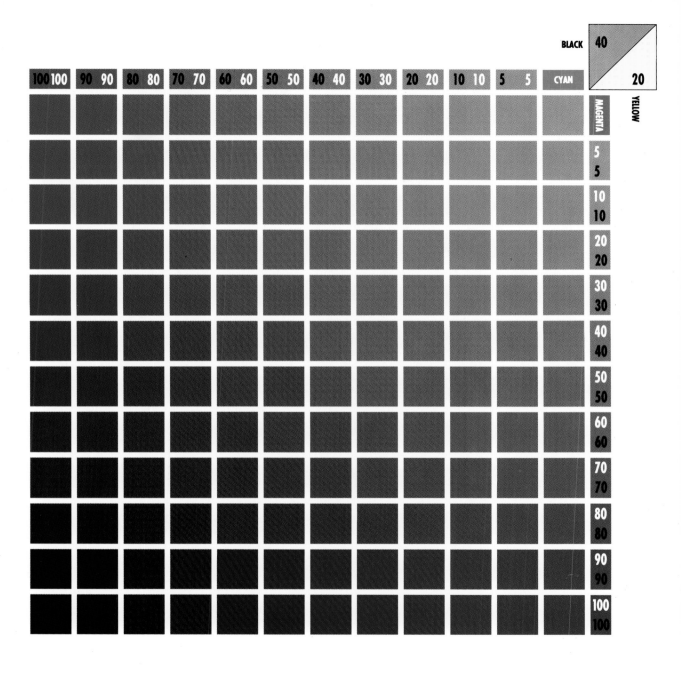

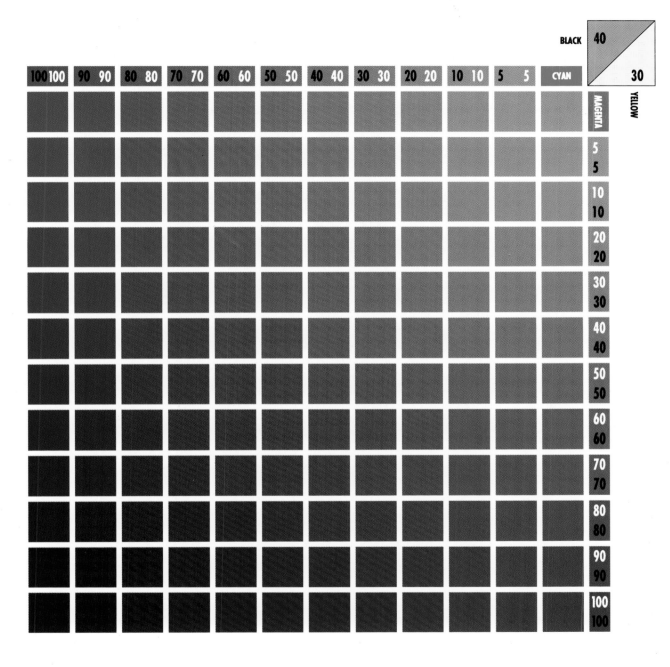

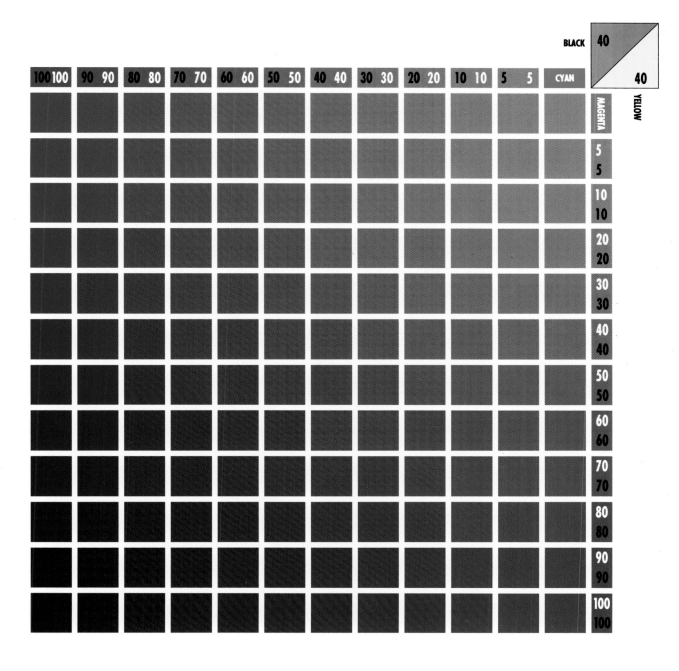

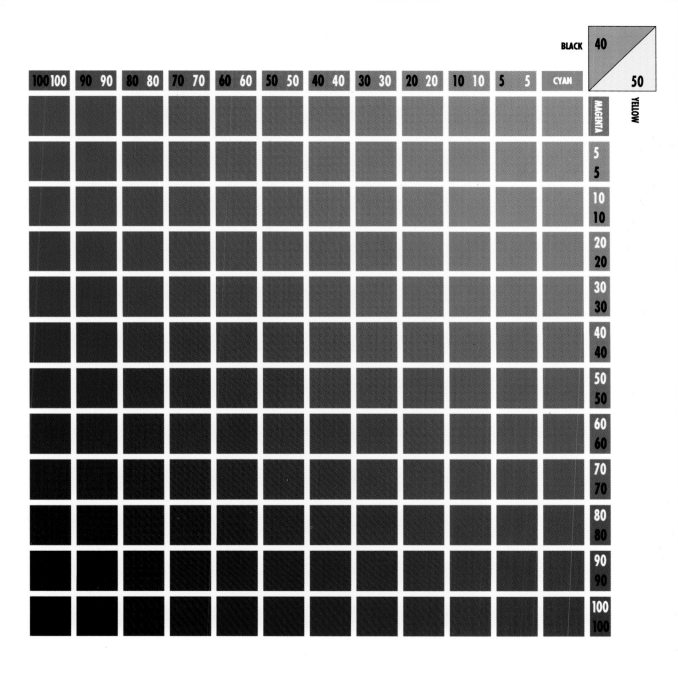

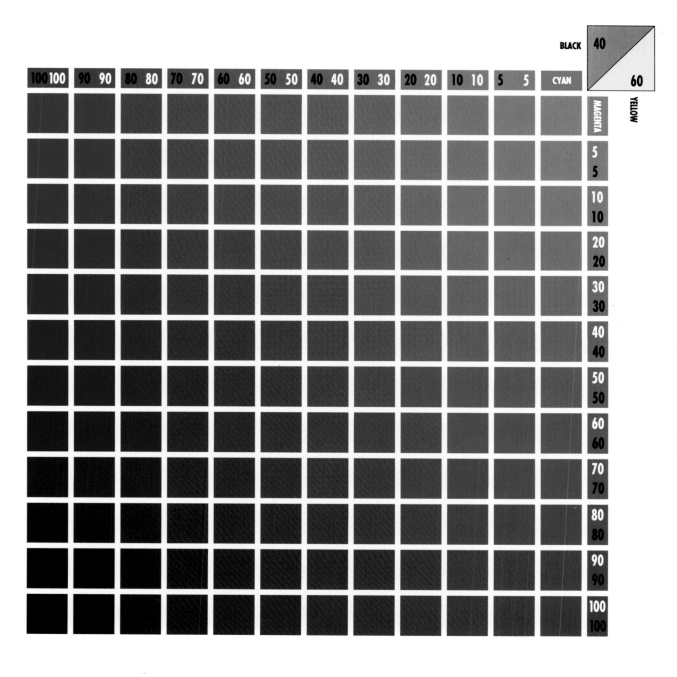

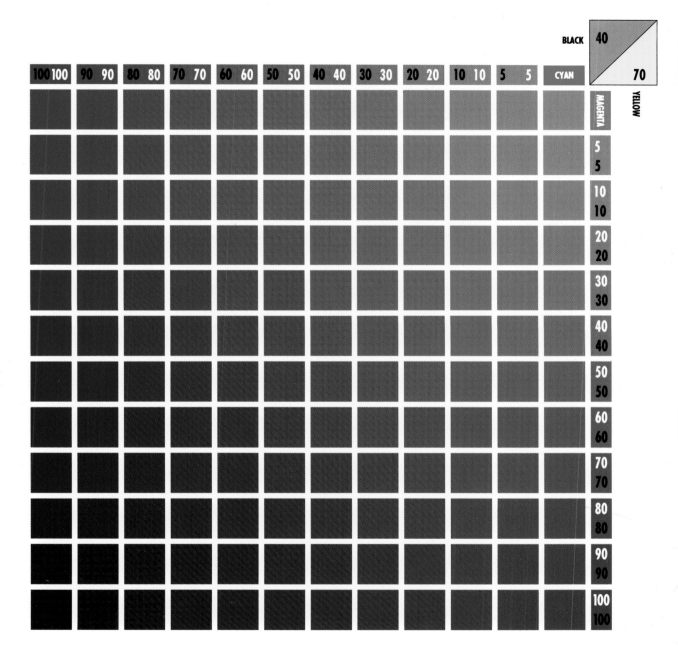

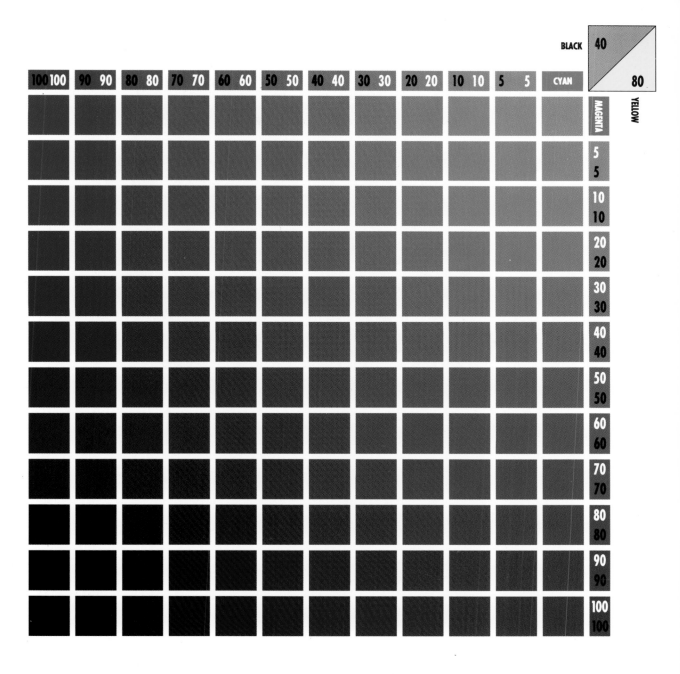

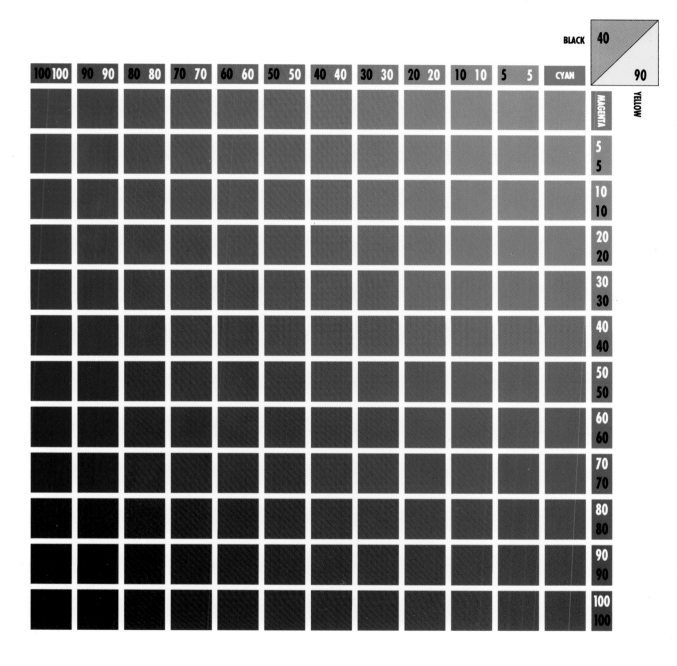

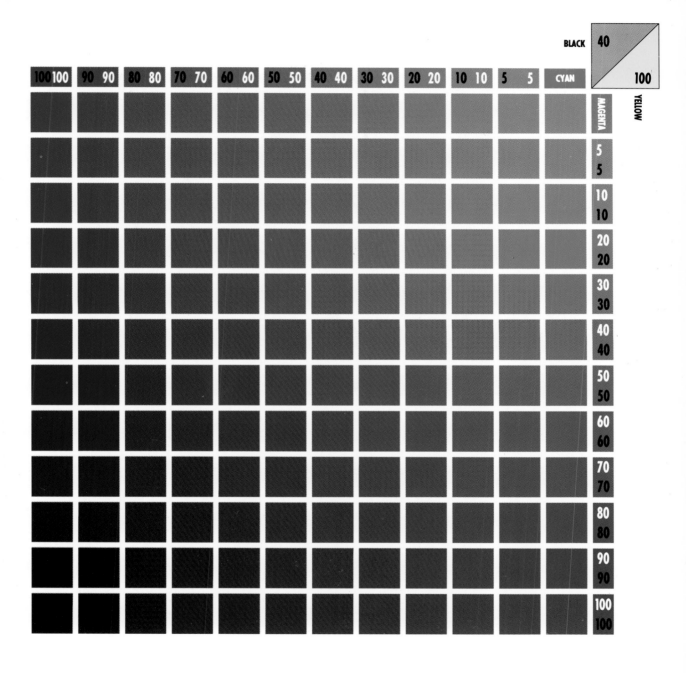

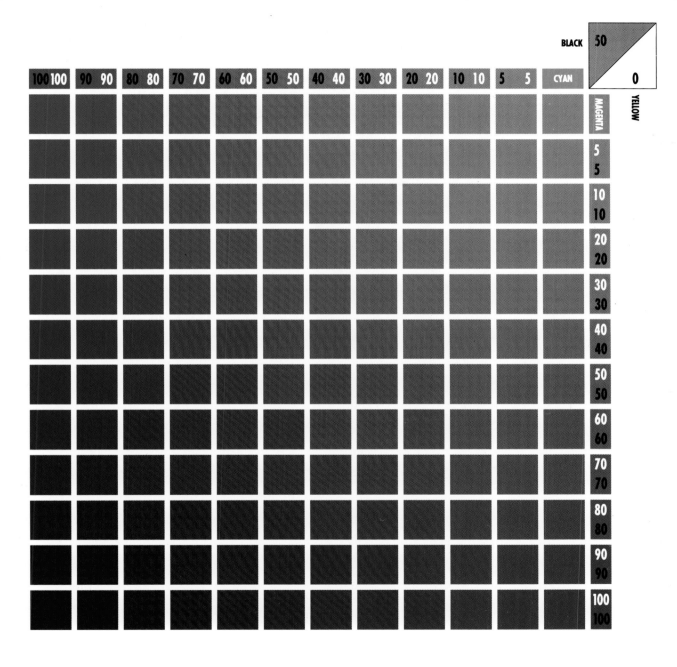

BLACK												50
												5

YELLOW

100 100	90 90	80 80	70 70	60 60	50 50	40 40	30 30	20 20	10 10	5 5	CYAN	MAGENTA
												5 5
												10 10
												20 20
												30 30
												40 40
												50 50
												60 60
												70 70
												80 80
												90 90
												100 100

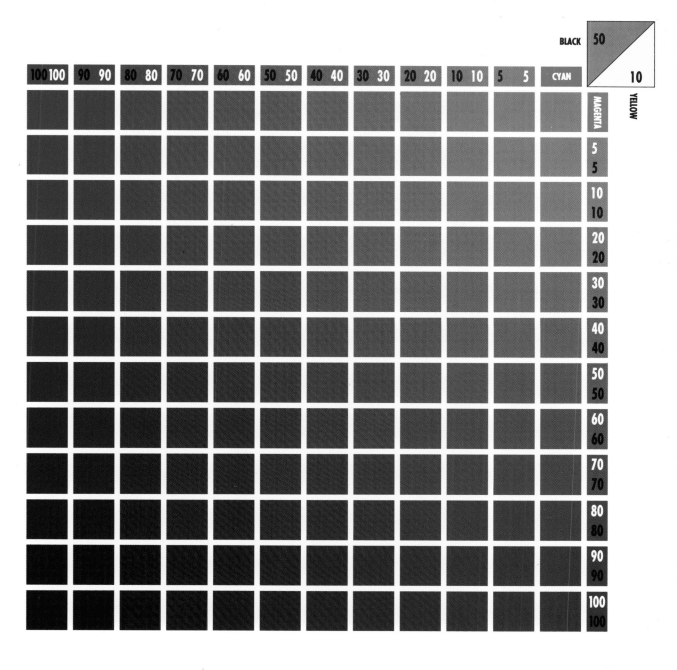

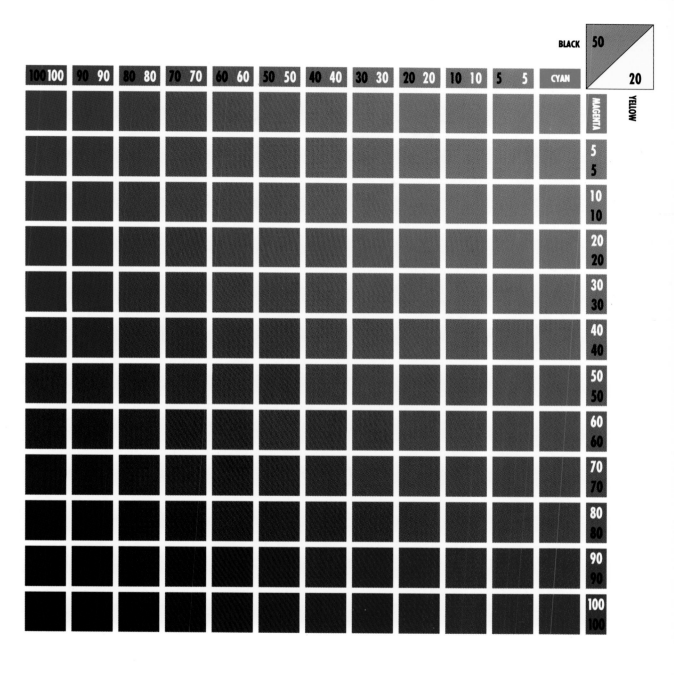

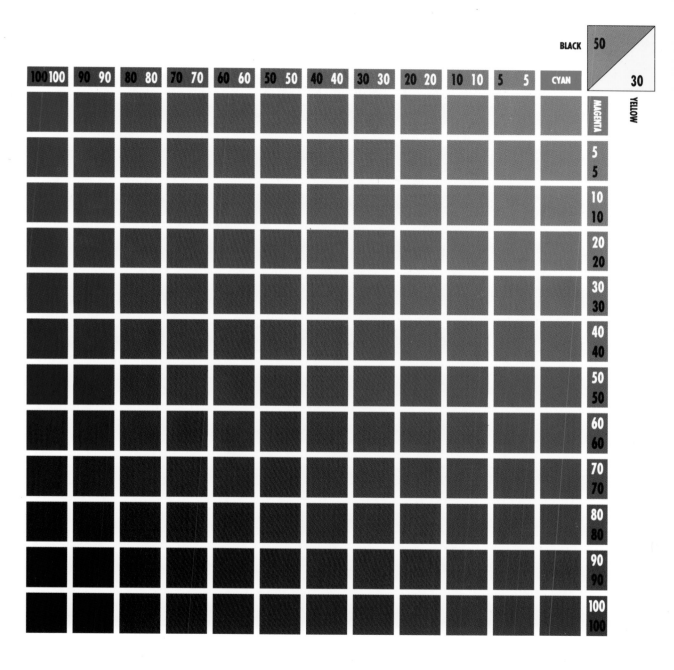

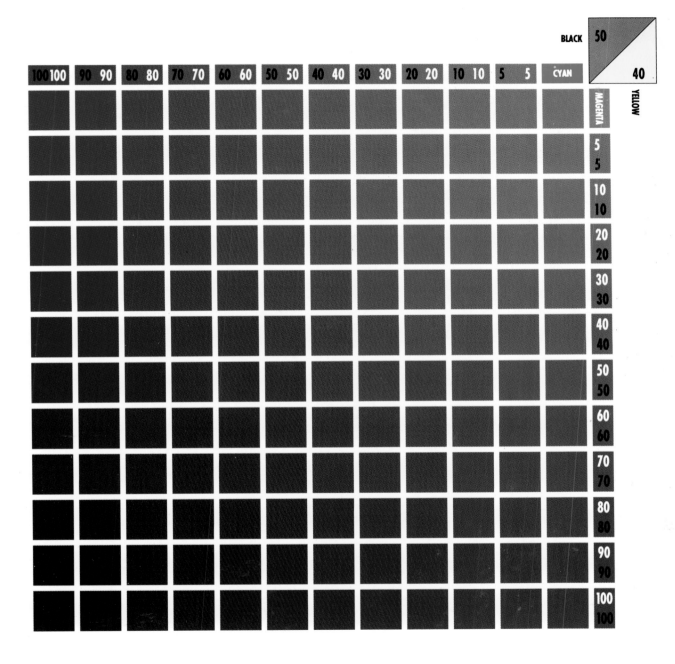

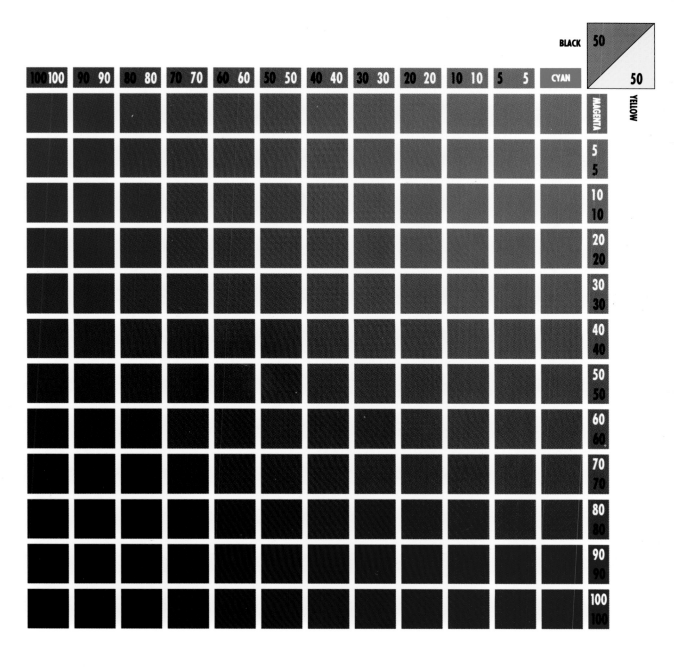

BLACK 50 / 60 YELLOW

100 100	90 90	80 80	70 70	60 60	50 50	40 40	30 30	20 20	10 10	5 5	CYAN	MAGENTA
												5 5
												10 10
												20 20
												30 30
												40 40
												50 50
												60 60
												70 70
												80 80
												90 90
												100 100

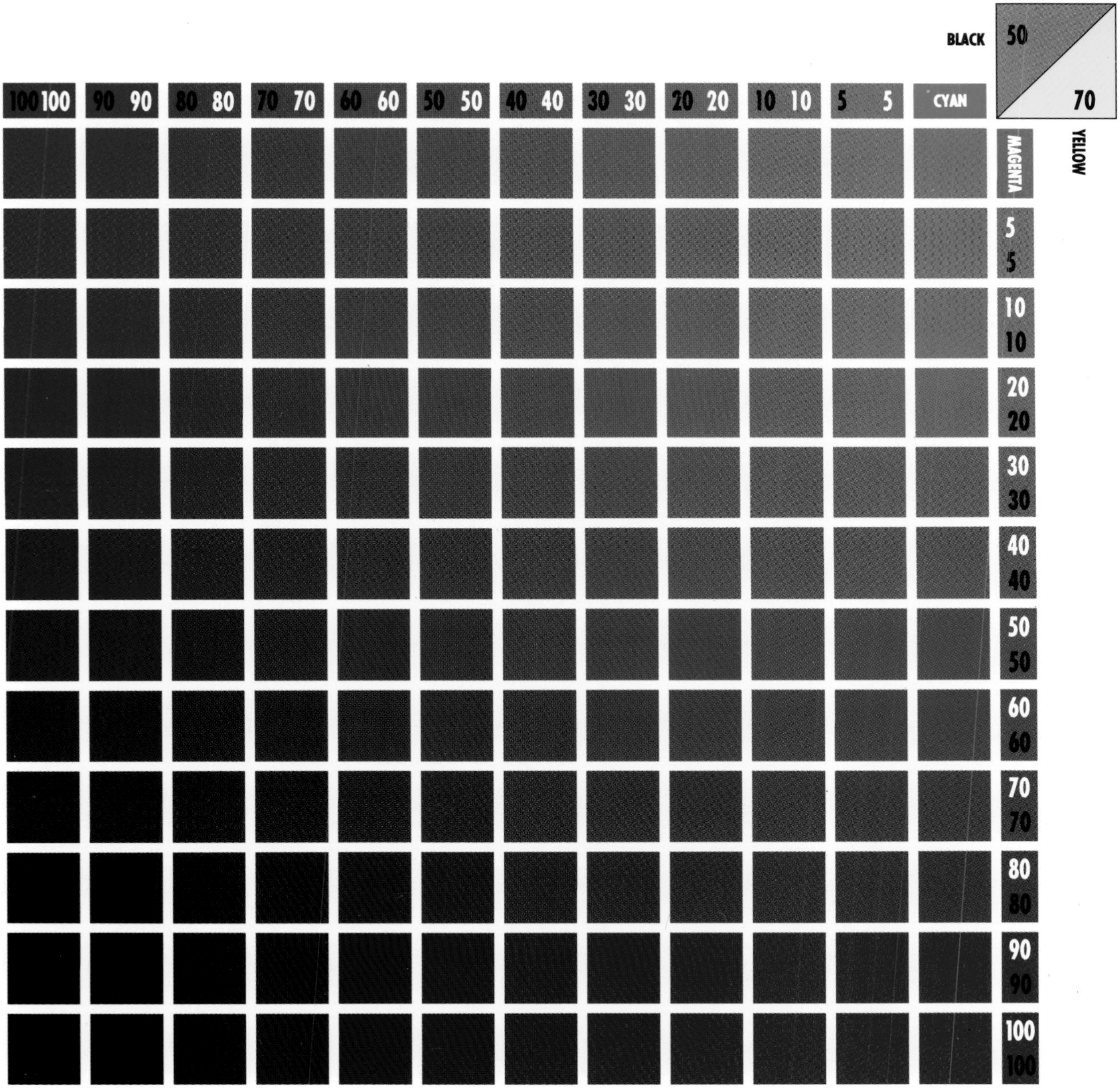
BLACK
50
70
YELLOW
CYAN
MAGENTA
100 100
90 90
80 80
70 70
60 60
50 50
40 40
30 30
20 20
10 10
5 5
5 5
10 10
20 20
30 30
40 40
50 50
60 60
70 70
80 80
90 90
100 100

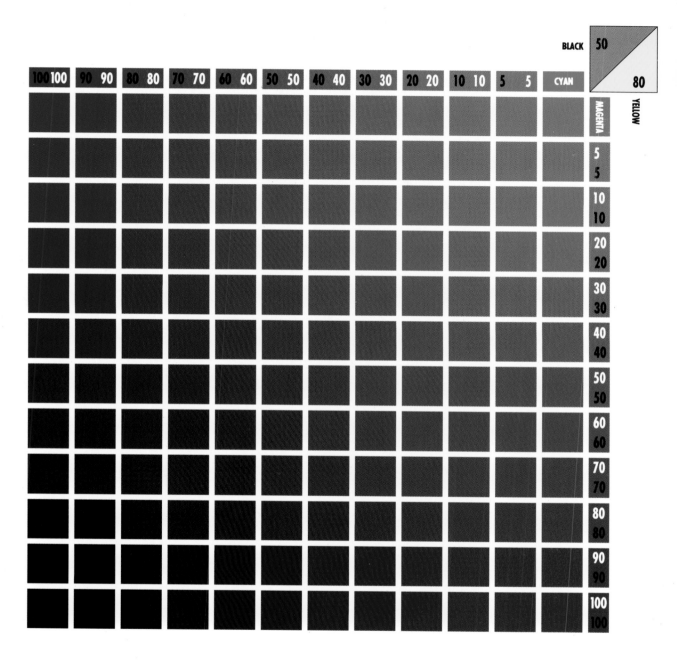

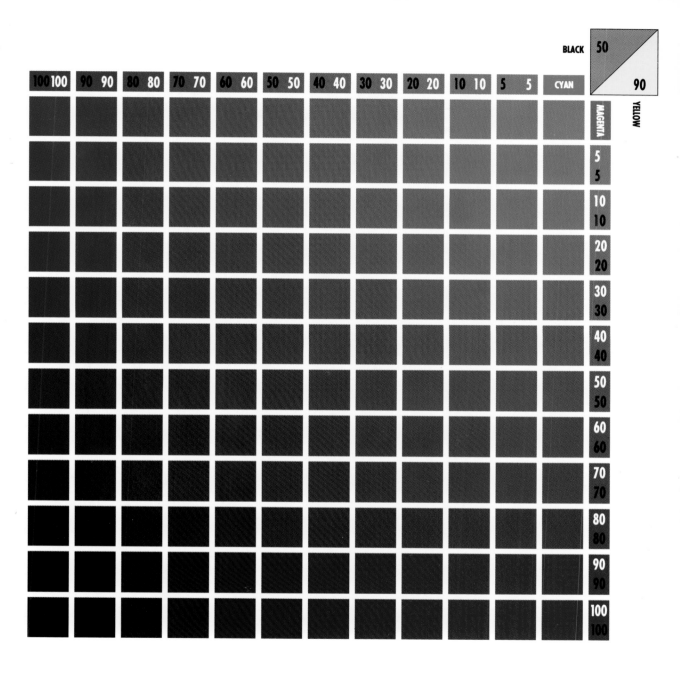

BLACK													50
													100

YELLOW

100 100	90 90	80 80	70 70	60 60	50 50	40 40	30 30	20 20	10 10	5 5	CYAN

| MAGENTA |
| 5 5 |
| 10 10 |
| 20 20 |
| 30 30 |
| 40 40 |
| 50 50 |
| 60 60 |
| 70 70 |
| 80 80 |
| 90 90 |
| 100 100 |

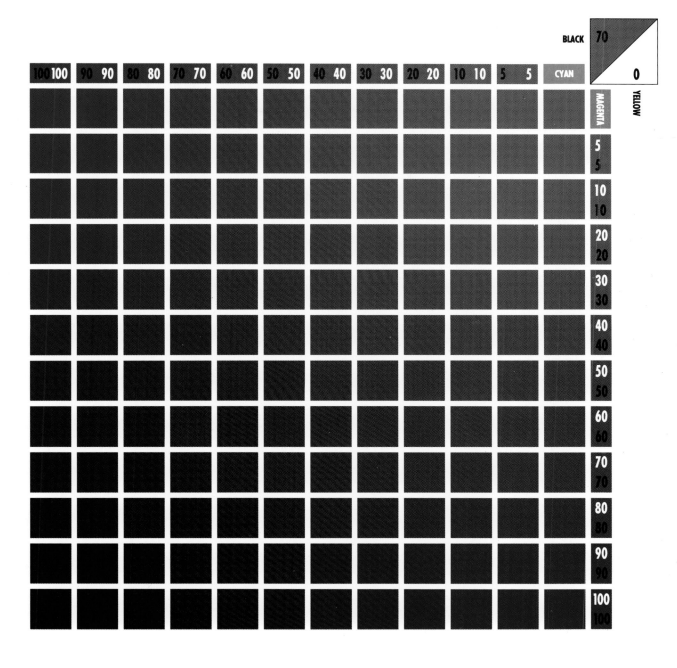

100	100	90	90	80	80	70	70	60	60	50	50	40	40	30	30	20	20	10	10	5	5	CYAN	BLACK 70

BLACK 70 / 5 YELLOW

MAGENTA

5 5

10 10

20 20

30 30

40 40

50 50

60 60

70 70

80 80

90 90

100 100

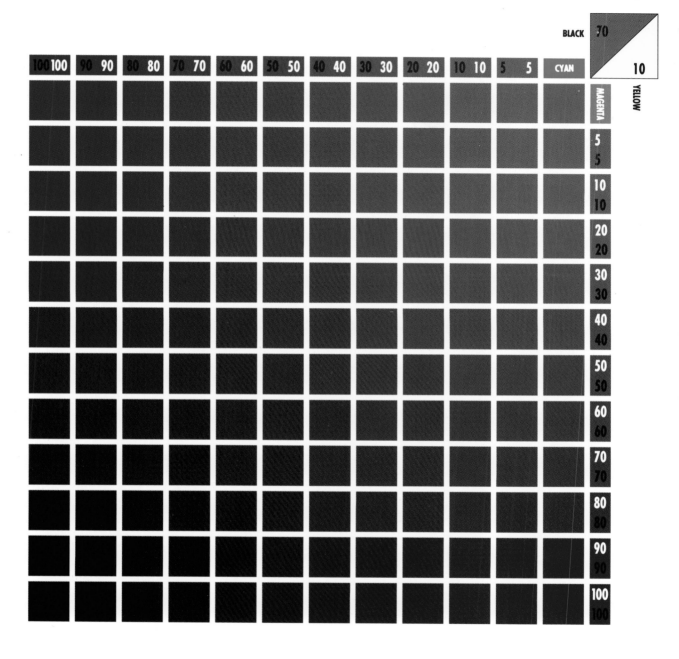

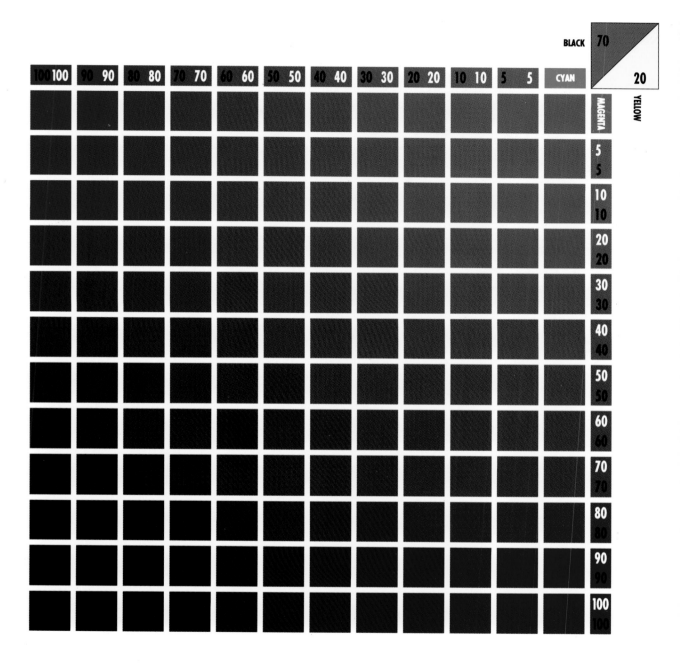

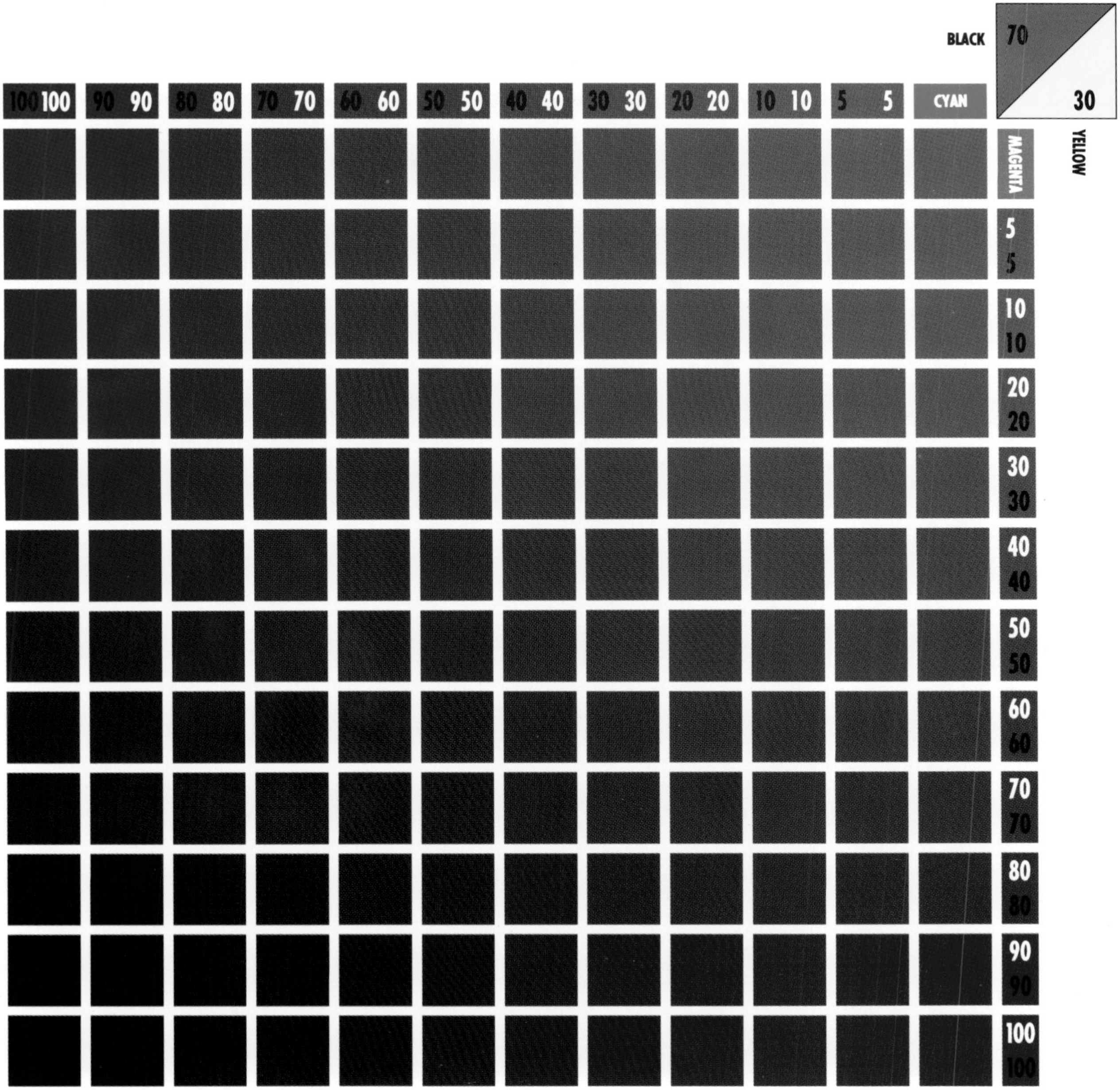
BLACK
70
30
YELLOW
100 100
90 90
80 80
70 70
60 60
50 50
40 40
30 30
20 20
10 10
5 5
CYAN
MAGENTA
5 5
10 10
20 20
30 30
40 40
50 50
60 60
70 70
80 80
90 90
100 100

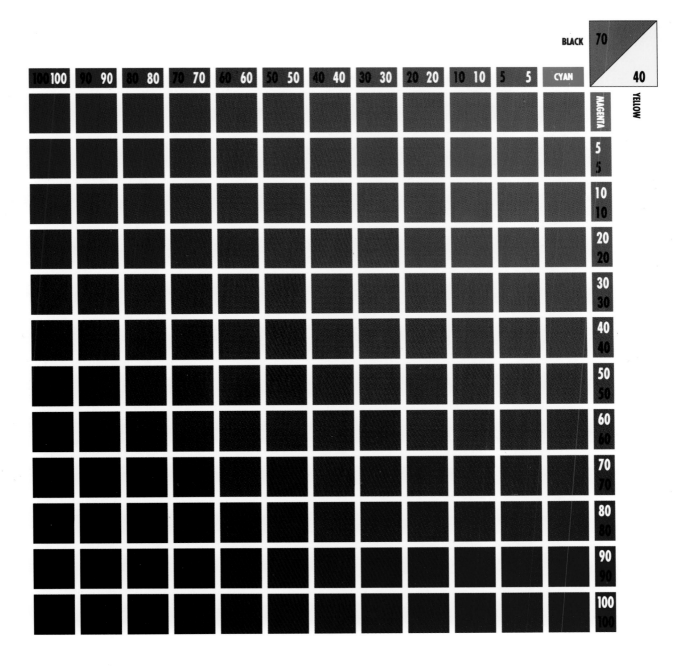

BLACK 70 / 50 YELLOW

100 100	90 90	80 80	70 70	60 60	50 50	40 40	30 30	20 20	10 10	5 5	CYAN	MAGENTA
												5 5
												10 10
												20 20
												30 30
												40 40
												50 50
												60 60
												70 70
												80 80
												90 90
												100 100

BLACK 70

YELLOW 60

| 100 100 | 90 90 | 80 80 | 70 70 | 60 60 | 50 50 | 40 40 | 30 30 | 20 20 | 10 10 | 5 5 | CYAN | MAGENTA |

| 5 5 |
| 10 10 |
| 20 20 |
| 30 30 |
| 40 40 |
| 50 50 |
| 60 60 |
| 70 70 |
| 80 80 |
| 90 90 |
| 100 100 |

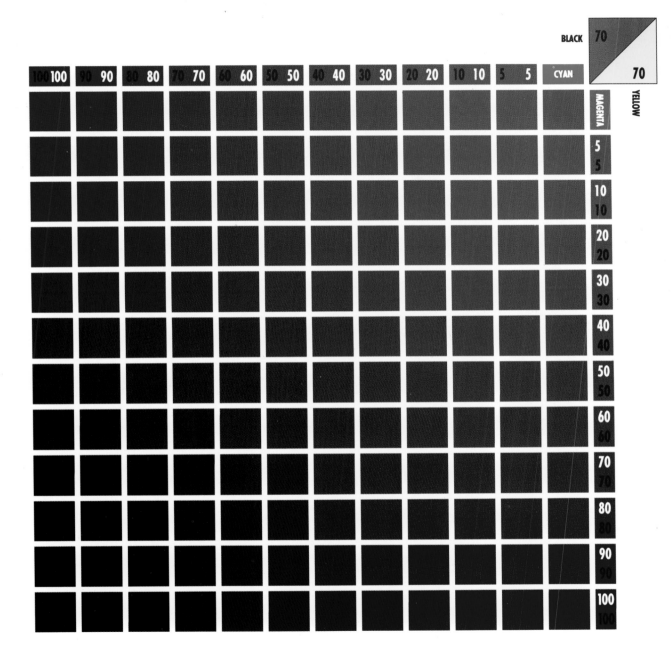

BLACK 70

80 YELLOW

| 100 100 | 90 90 | 80 80 | 70 70 | 60 60 | 50 50 | 40 40 | 30 30 | 20 20 | 10 10 | 5 5 | CYAN |

MAGENTA

5 5

10 10

20 20

30 30

40 40

50 50

60 60

70 70

80 80

90 90

100 100

BLACK 70

CYAN 90

YELLOW

| 100 100 | 90 90 | 80 80 | 70 70 | 60 60 | 50 50 | 40 40 | 30 30 | 20 20 | 10 10 | 5 5 | CYAN | MAGENTA |

100 100	90 90	80 80	70 70	60 60	50 50	40 40	30 30	20 20	10 10	5 5	CYAN	MAGENTA
												5 5
												10 10
												20 20
												30 30
												40 40
												50 50
												60 60
												70 70
												80 80
												90 90
												100 100